# AT A GLANCE

**Serendipity House / P.O. Box 1012 / Littleton, CO 80160**
TOLL FREE 1-800-525-9563 / www.serendipityhouse.com

SECOND EDITION

00  01  02  / **201 series • CHG** / 5  4

**PROJECT ENGINEER:**
Lyman Coleman

**WRITING TEAM:**
Richard Peace, Lyman Coleman, Andrew Sloan, Cathy Tardif

**PRODUCTION TEAM:**
Christopher Werner, Sharon Penington, Erika Tiepel

**COVER PHOTO:**
© 1998 Bill Ross / Westlight

## CORE VALUES

**Community:** The purpose of this curriculum is to build community within the body of believers around Jesus Christ.

**Group Process:** To build community, the curriculum must be designed to take a group through a step-by-step process of sharing your story with one another.

**Interactive Bible Study:** To share your "story," the approach to Scripture in the curriculum needs to be open-ended and right brain—to "level the playing field" and encourage everyone to share.

**Developmental Stages:** To provide a healthy program in the life cycle of a group, the curriculum needs to offer courses on three levels of commitment: (1) Beginner Stage—low-level entry, high structure, to level the playing field; (2) Growth Stage—deeper Bible study, flexible structure, to encourage group accountability; (3) Discipleship Stage—in-depth Bible study, open structure, to move the group into high gear.

**Target Audiences:** To build community throughout the culture of the church, the curriculum needs to be flexible, adaptable and transferable into the structure of the average church.

## ACKNOWLEDGMENTS

To Zondervan Bible Publishers
for permission to use
the NIV text,
*The Holy Bible, New International Bible Society.*
© 1973, 1978, 1984 by International Bible Society.
Used by permission of Zondervan Bible Publishers.

# Questions & Answers

**STAGE**

**1. What stage in the life cycle of a small group is this course designed for?**

Turn to the first page of the center section of this book. There you will see that this 201 course is designed for the second stage of a small group. In the Serendipity "Game Plan" for the multiplication of small groups, your group is in the Growth Stage.

**GOALS**

**2. What are the goals of a 201 study course?**

As shown on the second page of the center section (page M2), the focus in this second stage is equally balanced between Bible Study, Group Building, and Mission / Multiplication.

**BIBLE STUDY**

201

**3. What is the approach to Bible Study in this course?**

Take a look at page M3 of the center section. The objective in a 201 course is to discover what a book of the Bible, or a series of related Scripture passages, has to say to our lives today. We will study each passage seriously, but with a strong emphasis on practical application to daily living.

**THREE-STAGE LIFE CYCLE OF A GROUP**

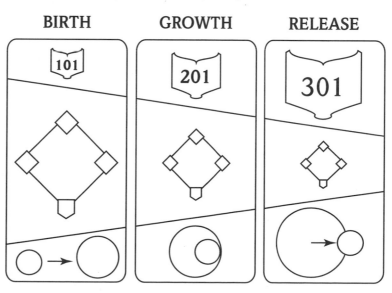

BIRTH          GROWTH          RELEASE

**GROUP BUILDING**

**4. What is the meaning of the baseball diamond on pages M2 and M3 in relation to Group Building?**

Every Serendipity course includes group building. First base is where we share our own stories; second base means affirming one another's stories; third base is sharing our personal needs; and home plate is deeply caring for each others' needs. In this 201 course we will continue "checking in" with each other and holding each other accountable to live the Christian life.

**MISSION / MULTIPLICATION**

**5. What is the mission of a 201 group?**

The mission of this 201 Covenant group is to discover the future leaders for starting a new group. (See graph on the previous page.) During this course, you will be challenged to identify three people and let this team use the Bible Study time to practice their skills. The center section will give you more details.

**THE EMPTY CHAIR**

**6. How do we fill "the empty chair"?**

First, pull up an empty chair during the group's prayer time and ask God to bring a new person to the group to fill it. Second, have everyone make a prospect list of people they could invite and keep this list on their refrigerator until they have contacted all those on their list.

**AGENDA**

**7. What is the agenda for our group meetings?**

A three-part agenda is found at the beginning of each session. Following the agenda and the recommended amount of time will keep your group on track and will keep the three goals of Bible Study, Group Building, and Mission / Multiplication in balance.

## THE FEARLESS FOURSOME

If you have more than seven people at a meeting, Serendipity recommends you divide into groups of 4 for the Bible Study. Count off around the group: "one, two, one, two, etc."—and have the "ones" move quickly to another room for the Bible Study. Ask one person to be the leader and follow the directions for the Bible Study time. After 30 minutes, the Group Leader will call "Time" and ask all groups to come together for the Caring Time.

**ICE-BREAKERS**

8. *How do we decide what ice-breakers to use to begin the meetings?*

   Page M7 of the center section contains an index of ice-breakers in four categories: (1) those for getting acquainted in the first session or when a new person comes to a meeting; (2) those for the middle sessions to help you report in to your group; (3) those for the latter sessions to affirm each other and assign roles in preparation for starting a new group in the future; and (4) those for evaluating and reflecting in the final session.

**GROUP COVENANT**

9. *What is a group covenant?*

   A group covenant is a "contract" that spells out your expectations and the ground rules for your group. It's very important that your group discuss these issues—preferably as part of the first session (see also page M32 in the center section).

**GROUND RULES**

10. *What are the ground rules for the group?* (Check those you agree upon.)

    ❏ PRIORITY: While you are in the course, you give the group meetings priority.

    ❏ PARTICIPATION: Everyone participates and no one dominates.

    ❏ RESPECT: Everyone is given the right to their own opinion and all questions are encouraged and respected.

    ❏ CONFIDENTIALITY: Anything that is said in the meeting is never repeated outside the meeting.

    ❏ EMPTY CHAIR: The group stays open to new people at every meeting.

    ❏ SUPPORT: Permission is given to call upon each other in time of need—even in the middle of the night.

    ❏ ADVICE GIVING: Unsolicited advice is not allowed.

    ❏ MISSION: We agree to do everything in our power to start a new group as our mission (see center section).

# Introduction to Galatians

## Audience

Paul tells us he is writing "to the churches in Galatia" (1:2). But where are these churches located? This is a problem, because in 25 B.C. the Romans created a new imperial province that they named Galatia. This new province was made up of the original kingdom of Galatia plus a new region to the south, forged out of territory originally belonging to six other regions. So when a first-century writer speaks of Galatia, it is not always clear whether he is referring to the original territory in the north, or the new province extending southward. In these notes, though scholarly opinion is divided at this point, the view is taken that Paul was writing to the churches he planted in South Galatia (Pisidian Antioch, Iconium, Lystra, and Derbe) during his first missionary journey described in Acts 13–14.

## Date

The date of Paul's epistle depends on whether he was writing to churches in North or South Galatia. If Paul had been writing to congregations in North Galatia, the letter could not have been written before his third missionary expedition (after the journey mentioned in Acts 16:6 and 18:23, around A.D. 55). On the other hand, if Paul were writing to the churches in the southern region, as we are assuming, the epistle to the Galatians is his earliest letter (written in A.D. 48 or 49), possibly while he was in Syrian Antioch just prior to the Council in Jerusalem (Acts 15:6–21).

## The Issue

Paul was furious and he didn't care who knew it. "You foolish Galatians!" he cried, "who has bewitched you?" (3:1). He felt so strongly because the issue he was addressing in this letter was not a minor matter of church policy. It struck right to the heart of the Gospel.

Apparently some legalistic Jewish-Christians (Judaizers) had been stirring up trouble. They had twisted the Gospel into something Jesus never intended, and then they had cast aspersions on Paul. "Who is that fellow, anyway? He wasn't one of the Twelve. He is a self-appointed apostle. No wonder he left out some crucial parts of the message. Let us set you straight. ..." And the Galatians were taken in, so it seems. Paul wrote, "I am astonished that you are so quickly deserting the one who called you by the grace of Christ and are turning to a different gospel" (1:6).

What were the Judaizers saying? At first glance, they seemed to be adding only a little to the message. "Believe in Christ," they were saying (they were Christians), "but also be circumcised" (6:12). Now to be circumcised was not such a high requirement, but Paul saw the implications. If the Galatians let themselves be circumcised, it would be but the first step back to keeping the whole Law (5:3). This is slavery (4:9). This is bondage (5:1). This is not the Gospel. The Gospel is that salvation is a free gift, by grace. If you add anything else to grace, salvation is no longer free. It then becomes a matter of doing the "other thing."

## Theme

The core issue in Galatians is justification. How does a person gain right standing before God? The Judaizers said that Christ (grace) plus circumcision (law-keeping) equals right standing. Paul's equation was different: Christ (grace) plus *nothing else* equals right standing. Works are excluded from Paul's equation. "A man is not justified by observing the law, but by faith in Jesus Christ. So we, too, have put our faith in Christ Jesus that we may be justified by faith in Christ and not by observing the law, because by observing the law no one will be justified" (2:16). This key verse sums up Paul's argument.

## The Implications

To the modern reader, it may seem at times as if Paul is getting worked up over a relatively small issue. After all, the important thing is to believe in Jesus, and all the parties agreed to that. But in fact, as history demonstrated, this issue was profound. Paul's concerns were more than validated. The underlying issue related to the universality of Christianity. Was Christianity for all people in all cultures (as Paul was arguing), or was it only a Jewish sect? To be a Christian, did you first have to become a Jew (which is the implication of the Judaizers' argument)? Did you have to accept Jewish customs, live a Jewish lifestyle, and submit to Jewish laws? If so (if the Judaizers had won), Christianity would probably have died out in the first century.

As we know, Christianity did not disappear along with all the Palestinian sects. Rather, the church was able to expand into the Greco-Roman world because the Gospel was truly universal. It was not tied to temple sacrifice and the Law of Moses, about which most pagans neither knew nor cared. The Judaizers wanted a Christianity circumscribed by Jewish exclusiveness, taboos, and customs—in which, by force, Gentile believers would always be second-class citizens. Paul fought this with vehemence and passion, as had other believers from Stephen

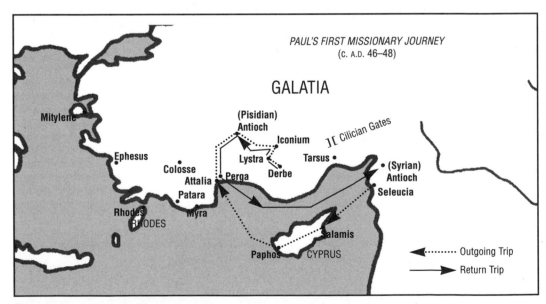

PAUL'S FIRST MISSIONARY JOURNEY
(C. A.D. 46–48)

GALATIA

Mitylene

(Pisidian) Antioch

Iconium    ][ Cilician Gates

Ephesus

Lystra    Tarsus •

Colosse

Attalia    Perga    Derbe    • (Syrian) Antioch

Patara    Seleucia

Rhodes    Myra

RHODES

Salamis

Paphos    CYPRUS

◄········ Outgoing Trip

◄———— Return Trip

onward; so Christianity became the transcultural world religion Christ had intended (Matt. 28:19–20).

## The Relationship Between Galatians and Romans

It is obvious that there is a close thematic connection between Galatians and Romans. Galatians appears to be Paul's first attempt at wrestling with the issue of justification by faith alone. Paul does so in the context of having to deal with a local problem. Romans, on the other hand, is a more studied consideration of the same issue. It is an eloquent, carefully stated, logical argument, which stands as one of the finest pieces of theological writing ever penned. Paul lifts the core of his argument from Galatians and shapes and refines it into a theological whole in Romans. As J.B. Lightfoot wrote: "The Epistle to the Galatians stands in relation to the Roman letter, as the rough model to the finished statue" (*St. Paul's Epistle to the Galatians*, p. 49).

## Structure

After a terse greeting (1:1–5) and pronouncement of anathema against the troublemakers (1:6–10), Paul launches into his first major theme: his *personal defense*, in which he deals with the charge that he is not a real apostle (1:11–2:21). This is followed by a *doctrinal defense*, in which he shows that Christianity lived under the Law is inferior to Christianity lived by faith (3:1–4:31). On the basis of these two arguments, he then shows what true Christian freedom is (5:1–6:10), ending with an unusual conclusion written in his own hand (6:11–18).

# 1 Salutation—Galatians 1:1–5

## THREE-PART AGENDA

**ICE-BREAKER**
15 Minutes

**BIBLE STUDY**
30 Minutes

**CARING TIME**
15–45 Minutes

>  *LEADER: Be sure to read pages 3–5 in the front of this book, and go over the ground rules on page 5 with the group in this first session. See page M7 in the center section for a good ice-breaker. Have your group look at pages M1–M5 in the center section and fill out the team roster on page M5.*

## TO BEGIN THE BIBLE STUDY TIME
(Choose 1 or 2)

1. What letter or postcard have you received from the farthest distance?

2. How long are the letters you write: Short and sweet? Until writer's cramp sets in? What letters?!

3. What is the closest you have come to needing to be rescued? What happened?

## READ SCRIPTURE & DISCUSS
(If you don't have time for all the questions in this section, conclude the Bible Study [30 min.] by answering question #8.)

1. When have you had to defend your stand on an issue? How did it turn out?

2. What, according to Paul's claim in verse 1, gives him the right to be heard (see last note on v. 1)?

3. PAST: What did Jesus Christ voluntarily do for Paul and the Galatians—and us (v. 4)?

**1** *Paul, an apostle—sent not from men nor by man, but by Jesus Christ and God the Father, who raised him from the dead—²and all the brothers with me,*

*To the churches in Galatia:*

*³Grace and peace to you from God our Father and the Lord Jesus Christ, ⁴who gave himself for our sins to rescue us from the present evil age, according to the will of our God and Father, ⁵to whom be glory for ever and ever. Amen.*

4. At what point in your life were you most aware of your need to be changed by Jesus Christ? What happened?

5. PRESENT: What ongoing spiritual blessings are available now (v. 3)?

6. What blessing or gift from God is most needed in your life right now?

7. FUTURE: What will God deservedly receive for the rest of time (v. 5)?

8. What spiritual commitment or goal do you feel God calling you to make for his honor and glory?

## CARING TIME

1. Have your group agree on its group covenant and ground rules (see page 5 in the front of this book).

2. Work on filling out your team roster (see page M5 in the center section.) Like any winning team, every position needs to be covered.

3. Who is someone you would like to invite to this group for next week?

*P.S. At the close, pass around your books and have everyone sign the Group Directory inside the front cover.*

Share prayer requests and close in prayer. Be sure to pray for "the empty chair" (p. 4).

**Summary.** This greeting is chilly in tone by comparison to other greetings sent to churches which Paul founded. The relationship between Paul and the Galatians is obviously strained at this point in time. He says nothing in praise of the Galatians' activities and, in fact, is quite defensive (since apparently they are questioning his authority as an apostle).

**1:1 *Paul.*** While some scholars dispute whether or not Paul actually wrote all the epistles traditionally assigned to him, virtually everyone accepts that he was the author of Galatians. In fact, Galatians is often used as the model by which to test the "genuineness" of other epistles.

***apostle.*** This New Testament word means "a special messenger," and was used at first to denote the Twelve who were originally chosen by Jesus. Very soon, however, the term became more inclusive, being applied first to Matthias who replaced Judas Iscariot (Acts 1:26) and then to others (Rom. 16:7; 1 Cor. 15:7–9) including Paul. The apostles were those individuals who were regarded as final authorities in matters of faith and practice.

***not from men ... but by Jesus.*** Paul emphasizes that his apostleship derives not from any human intermediary (as does, for example, the authority of the men in 2 Cor. 8:23 Paul calls "apostles of the church"—which is the literal translation of the verse). Rather his commission was received directly from the resurrected Christ on the Damascus road. This is important because apparently his opponents were giving out a different story in their attempt to demean his authority. The authority of a person is directly related to the authority of the one who does the commissioning. Hence when Paul speaks, he does so with Christ's authority.

**1:2 *To the churches.*** This was a circular letter sent primarily to the churches in Pisidian Antioch, Iconium, Lystra, and Derbe (Acts 13:14–14:23), though other congregations may have sprung up in the area by the time of its composition.

***Galatia.*** The Roman province of Galatia was located in what is now the central part of Turkey (see a Bible map). The original kingdom of Galatia in the north had been settled by Celtic tribespeople who had migrated from the Danube basin in Central Europe to Asia Minor. (The Celts also migrated into Gaul and Britain.)

**1:3 *Grace and peace.*** These words are typically used by Paul to begin a letter, pointing to God's goodwill toward humanity expressed in the saving work of Christ (grace), and to the resultant quality of life with God that ensues for those who have opened themselves to the operation of this divine grace (peace).

> *The authority of a person is directly related to the authority of the one who does the commissioning. Hence when Paul speaks, he does so with Christ's authority.*

**1:4** "This is probably the earliest written statement in the New Testament about the significance of the death of Christ" (F. F. Bruce).

***gave himself.*** The idea is of voluntary sacrifice for a specific purpose.

***for our sins.*** A crucial phrase, indicating that this was not just the death of a martyr, but was rather an act of cosmic significance which made possible the forgiveness of sin (and hence opened the way for men and women back to God). Such a statement defining the purpose of Christ's death is often found in primitive summaries of the Gospel (1 Cor. 15:3).

***rescue.*** To be rescued from bondage is a key idea in the epistle. The word carries the idea of being delivered from the power of another, and is used elsewhere in the New Testament to describe the rescue of the Israelites from Egypt (Acts 7:34) and the release of Peter from prison and from Herod (Acts 12:11). Here it is used metaphorically to describe salvation by pointing to Christ's triumph over the bondage of evil.

*the present evil age.* There are two ages: "this age" which is evil and under Satan's control, and "the age to come" which was inaugurated when Christ came. Both ages run side by side at the moment. In becoming a Christian, a person is shifted, as it were, from one mode of reality into the other—escaping from the track that leads to ultimate death to that which gives eternal life.

**1:5** *to whom be glory.* A doxology in praise of God's deliverance.

## Paul ... The Controversial Apostle

It wasn't easy for Paul to be an apostle. It seems that right from the beginning he was a controversial figure. After he was converted on the Damascus Road, the first reaction of Christians to this news was skepticism and fear (Acts 9:13–14,26). They found it hard to believe that the fiery Saul who sought to take Christians prisoner (Acts 9:1–2) was now on their side. Then when he began his ministry, despite his success and despite the fact that his apostleship was certified by the original apostles themselves (Gal. 2:1–10), he still kept on having to defend his right to function as an apostle (e.g., 2 Cor. 10; Gal. 1:11–2:10). Two questions seemed to haunt him:

• Is he a real apostle?

• Does he preach the genuine Gospel?

These two questions may well have been in the minds of the Galatian Christians.

But Paul says a great deal in his brief introduction (1:1) to allay their suspicions, as he points out that he did not just decide one day to become an apostle. It was God himself who called him to this office. He simply responded in obedience.

Despite the rumors they might have heard, here was a genuine and humble man of God and not some pretend apostle who wanted merely to have power over them.

## How Greeks Began Their Letters

A lot of ancient Greek letters have been found by archaeologists. Most all of them begin in the same way—with the name of the sender(s) followed by the name(s) of the recipient(s) and then ending with a brief salutation, usually simply the word "Greetings." You can see this in the letter quoted in Acts 23:26: "Claudius Lysias, To His Excellency, Governor Felix: Greetings."

Paul "Christianizes" the standard greeting. Rather than simply saying "greetings" as the Romans did, he uses a slightly different word from the same Greek root, namely "grace." To this he adds the Greek version of the common Hebrew greeting "Shalom" or "peace." Thus he conveys in these two words, "grace and peace," the essence of the Christian Gospel: Grace freely given by God to sinners effects reconciliation or peace with God.

# 2 No Other Gospel—Galatians 1:6–10

5-30-2001

## THREE-PART AGENDA

**ICE-BREAKER**
15 Minutes

**BIBLE STUDY**
30 Minutes

**CARING TIME**
15–45 Minutes

---

 *LEADER: If there's a new person in your group in this session, start with an ice-breaker (see page M7 in the center section). Then begin the session with a word of prayer. If you have more than seven in your group, see the box about the "Fearless Foursome" on page 4. Count off around the group: "one, two, one, two, etc."—and have the "ones" move quickly to another room for the Bible Study.*

## TO BEGIN THE BIBLE STUDY TIME
(Choose 1 or 2)

1. What subject in high school or college was most confusing to you?

2. In major purchases (like vehicles), do you typically switch manufacturers or stay with the same one?

3. When you're upset with someone, do you usually give them a long lecture, a "piece of your mind," or the "silent treatment"?

## READ SCRIPTURE & DISCUSS
(If you don't have time for all the questions in this section, conclude the Bible Study [30 min.] by answering question #7.)

1. How do you respond to criticism: Take it to heart and try to change? Ignore it? Get upset? Lose sleep? Other?

2. How would you feel if a preacher began a sermon the way Paul begins the heart of this letter?

## No Other Gospel

*⁶I am astonished that you are so quickly deserting the one who called you by the grace of Christ and are turning to a different gospel— ⁷which is really no gospel at all. Evidently some people are throwing you into confusion and are trying to pervert the gospel of Christ. ⁸But even if we or an angel from heaven should preach a gospel other than the one we preached to you, let him be eternally condemned! ⁹As we have already said, so now I say again: If anybody is preaching to you a gospel other than what you accepted, let him be eternally condemned!*

*¹⁰Am I now trying to win the approval of men, or of God? Or am I trying to please men? If I were still trying to please men, I would not be a servant of Christ.*

3. What kind of "gospel" was being preached by those who Paul contends had led the Galatians astray (see "The Issue" on page 7)?

4. What does Paul say will happen to anyone who promotes and teaches a "gospel" other than that which Paul preached— the good news of grace (vv. 8–9)?

5. Who has been an "apostle Paul" in your life— someone who has made a significant contribution to your spiritual beginning or growth?

6. Have you ever strayed from your faith in Christ? What happened?

7. What can you do in the coming week to be more faithful to Christ and his Gospel?

## CARING TIME
(Choose 1 or 2 of these questions before closing in prayer. Be sure to pray for the empty chair.)

1. Who did you invite to the group this week? Who would you like to invite to the next meeting to fill "the empty chair"?

2. If you were to describe this past week of your life in terms of weather, what was it like: Sunny and warm? Cold? Scattered showers? Other? What is the forecast for the coming week?

3. How can the group pray for you this week?

*P.S. Add new group members to the Group Directory inside the front cover.*

**Summary.** Paul points out that there is only one version of the Gospel and he is astounded that the Galatians should depart from it, regardless of who the proclaimer might be. Such distorters are worthy of condemnation. For his part, he refuses to tailor his message to the whims of the audience.

**1:6 *astonished.*** Typically at this place in a letter, Paul would commend the church (e.g., Rom. 1:8; Phil. 1:3). But here he skips the praise altogether and launches straight into his remonstration, expressing indignation at the news that they have been persuaded by the teaching of the Judaizers.

***so quickly.*** Paul has scarcely returned from his first missionary journey and already the Galatians are turning away from the truth.

***deserting.*** The word means, literally, a removal from one place to another, as for example the bones of Abraham from Egypt to Shechem (Acts 7:16). The word can also be used for those who "change sides"—for example, army deserters.

***called.*** It was God who beckoned them to salvation and from whom they are now defecting (though Paul's opponents would not have seen it that way, preferring to think that they were calling people to the true way).

***grace.*** This pinpoints the nature of their *turning*— from a gospel of unmerited favor to a gospel of works.

***gospel.*** The proclamation of the good news that in the life, death and resurrection of Jesus, the kingdom of God has been made manifest and is open to all who by faith trust in his atoning work on the cross.

**1:7 *no gospel.*** A different gospel is really no gospel at all. It does not merit description as "good news." To be thrown back into bondage to the Law is, indeed, "bad news."

***throwing you into confusion.*** Some people are "troubling" the Galatians, "disturbing the peace" that ought to be found in the Gospel. The root word probably means seditious activity that would lead to desertion.

***pervert.*** The nature of the perversion will be made clear in chapter 5: Male Gentile converts are being urged to be circumcised as a precondition for acceptance by God. "This word means to transfer to a different opinion, hence to change the essential character of a thing. ... The idea is not merely a twisting of the Gospel, but of giving it an emphasis which is virtually transformed into something else" (Guthrie).

**1:8** What is crucial is the message, not the messenger. No matter who the messenger may be, that person and that message is to be rejected if it is different from that which brought salvation to the Galatians. It is the *Gospel of Christ,* not the gospel of Paul or anyone else.

> *The Gospel is the proclamation of the good news that in the life, death and resurrection of Jesus, the kingdom of God has been made manifest and is open to all who by faith trust in his atoning work on the cross.*

***eternally condemned.*** The Greek word is *anathema* and is related to the Hebrew idea of the "ban," i.e., that which is set apart to God, usually for destruction. It stands as the direct opposite to God's grace, and is used by Paul as a solemn calling down of judgment on these Judaizers.

**1:10 *now ... still.*** There is an implied criticism of Paul here. Apparently he was being charged with vacillation—saying one thing here, another there; acting this way now, but in a different fashion elsewhere. "Who can trust that sort of person?" the Judaizers would have been saying. But as Paul points out, his anathema in verse 9 is certainly not the language of a man-pleaser!

***win the approval.*** Literally, "persuade." In fact, Paul understood his mission to be one of persuasion (see 2 Cor. 5:11), and to urge individuals to be reconciled to God (2 Cor. 5:20). But while it was his role to persuade human beings, it was not his job to persuade God. In fact, the very thought was abhorrent. God was God and his will reigned. Only religious charlatans claimed to a superstitious audience that they could change God's mind.

**please men.** Men-pleasing (i.e., shifting his message and methods to gain their approval) was abhorrent to Paul (1 Thess. 2:4–6). So what Paul is saying is "that he persuades men, not God, and pleases God, not men; indeed, he pleases God by persuading men" (Bruce).

> *Right standing before God is a gift. One merely has to accept it; i.e., to believe that via the death and resurrection of Jesus this gift is offered and to trust that when God says we have right standing that indeed we do. The Christian, therefore, approaches the judgment seat with confidence and love because the verdict has already been rendered. They have been pardoned.*

## The Problem of Righteousness

For many first-century people THE ISSUE in life was how to get on the right side of the gods. The gods were understood to be powerful. They could bring great wealth, happiness, or success—or they could destroy you in the twinkling of an eye. And their power extended to the afterlife.

Gentiles sought the favor of the gods via a confusing host of religious systems, including the so-called "mystery religions" with their secret and bloody rites. Jews sought the favor of Jehovah via a complex system of behaviors and rituals. But neither Jew nor Greek had much confidence that they had succeeded in befriending God. The Jews, for example, would only know on the Judgment Day itself whether they had really kept more laws than they broke. It was in terror that they would approach the judgment seat of God.

This is why Paul is so excited about the Gospel. All the anxiety is now gone. The good news is out that a person does not have to do anything to win God's favor—neither behavioral nor ritual. Right standing before God is a *gift*. One merely has to accept it; i.e., to believe that via the death and resurrection of Jesus this gift is offered and to trust that when God says we have right standing that indeed we do. The Christian, therefore, approaches the judgment seat with confidence and love because the verdict has already been rendered. They have been pardoned. This news is still as astonishing today as it was in the first century.

6/16/2001

## THREE-PART AGENDA

| ICE-BREAKER | BIBLE STUDY | CARING TIME |
|---|---|---|
| 15 Minutes | 30 Minutes | 15–45 Minutes |

>  *LEADER: Remember to choose an appropriate ice-breaker if you have a new person at the meeting (see page M7 in the center section), and then begin with a prayer. If you have more than seven in your group, divide into groups of four for the Bible Study (see the box about the "Fearless Foursome" on page 4).*

## TO BEGIN THE BIBLE STUDY TIME
(Choose 1 or 2)

1. Where did you go on your last vacation? Where would you like to go next?

2. At age 18, what career were you preparing for or starting? How does that relate to your life now?

3. What church did you grow up in? What did your religious education consist of?

## READ SCRIPTURE & DISCUSS
(If you don't have time for all the questions in this section, conclude the Bible Study [30 min.] by answering question #7.)

1. What "revelation" or news has most dramatically affected your life?

2. What is the revelation that Paul received from Jesus Christ?

3. How did this revelation change Paul's life? What was Paul called by God to do (vv. 15–16)?

4. How did Paul now view his Jewish traditions? What church traditions help you in your faith? Which ones may hinder your faith?

## Paul Called by God

*[11]I want you to know, brothers, that the gospel I preached is not something that man made up. [12]I did not receive it from any man, nor was I taught it; rather, I received it by revelation from Jesus Christ.*

*[13]For you have heard of my previous way of life in Judaism, how intensely I persecuted the church of God and tried to destroy it. [14]I was advancing in Judaism beyond many Jews of my own age and was extremely zealous for the traditions of my fathers. [15]But when God, who set me apart from birth[a] and called me by his grace, was pleased [16]to reveal his Son in me so that I might preach him among the Gentiles, I did not consult any man, [17]nor did I go up to Jerusalem to see those who were apostles before I was, but I went immediately into Arabia and later returned to Damascus.*

*[18]Then after three years, I went up to Jerusalem to get acquainted with Peter[b] and stayed with him fifteen days. [19]I saw none of the other apostles—only James, the Lord's brother. [20]I assure you before God that what I am writing you is no lie. [21]Later I went to Syria and Cilicia. [22]I was personally unknown to the churches of Judea that are in Christ. [23]They only heard the report: "The man who formerly persecuted us is now preaching the faith he once tried to destroy." [24]And they praised God because of me.*

[a]15 Or *from my mother's womb*          [b]18 Greek *Cephas*

---

5. How does your past affect your present life? What do you need to put behind you and know you are forgiven?

6. How have you seen God change lives today as he did with Paul?

7. What do you feel called by God to do with your life?

## CARING TIME

(Choose 1 or 2 of these questions before closing in prayer. Be sure to pray for the empty chair.)

1. How comfortable do you feel sharing your needs and struggles with this group?

2. Does everyone in the group have a position on the team roster (review p. M5)?

3. How can your "brothers and sisters" lift you up in prayer this week?

**Summary.** Paul recounts how he came to be an apostle, as he seeks to defend himself against the charge that he was not really an apostle and therefore unqualified to teach the true Gospel. His point is that his commission came directly from God (vv. 11–17), though later it was recognized by the leaders of the Jerusalem church (1:18–2:10).

**1:11** Paul first states what the Gospel is not. It is not a product of intellectual musings, nor the conclusion of a philosophical system, nor even the logical outcome of centuries of Jewish thought.

> *Because he had been so zealous for Judaism, there was no one less likely than Paul to abandon the way of the Law. This could only have come about as the result of a direct revelation.*
>
> *He even evokes a solemn oath to make his point; his message was from God, not men.*

**brothers.** Paul's word for fellow Christians. Even though he has harsh words for the Galatians, they are still part of the family of faith. His words come with the awareness of this relationship, and are laced with love for them.

**1:12 *revelation.*** Literally, "an opening up of what was previously hidden." Paul had certainly heard the "facts" of the Gospel prior to his conversion, but he had violently rejected them as blasphemous. It was only after Jesus Christ revealed the truth and meaning of these facts to him on the Damascus road that he accepted the Gospel.

**1:13–24** Because he had been so zealous for Judaism, there was no one less likely than Paul to abandon the way of the Law. This could only have come about as the result of a direct revelation. Thus, Paul verifies his assertion in verse 12 that he received the Gospel by revelation. He has pointed out that only in that way would he as a passionately fanatical Jew have come to believe in Jesus. He has also pointed out where he went after his conversion, to show that he was not influenced by the Jerusalem leaders. He even evokes a solemn oath (v. 20) to make his point; his message was from God, not men.

**1:13 *For you have heard.*** Apparently, as part of their campaign to discredit Paul, the Judaizers had been circulating rumors of his violent action toward the church when he was a Pharisee. "Can you trust a person who did things like that?" is the implication of this charge.

**how intensely.** Literally, beyond measure, excessively or violently.

**I persecuted.** See Acts 7:58–8:3; 26:11.

**1:14 *zealous.*** Zeal was highly praised by the Jews as a religious virtue (Num. 25:11–13).

**traditions of my fathers.** In particular, the oral law developed over the years to explain and apply the Old Testament, taught to Paul in the school of Gamaliel (Acts 22:3).

**1:15 *set me apart from birth.*** Paul's experience is similar to that of Old Testament prophets. See Isaiah 49:1–6 and Jeremiah 1:5.

**1:16 *among the Gentiles.*** With Paul's conversion came also his commission to preach to the Gentiles (Acts 9:15). In encountering Christ, he came to the realization that the Law was bankrupt (insofar as its ability to save anyone). Thus, there was no barrier preventing Gentiles from coming to the all-sufficient Christ.

**1:17** Apparently the Judaizers had been saying that after his conversion Paul had gone to Jerusalem and there received instructions about the Gospel (including the requirement to be circumcised), but then later Paul went his own way and started teaching a law-free Gospel. In rebuttal Paul denies once again (see also v. 12) that he was so instructed.

**go up to Jerusalem.** Jerusalem was the headquarters of the Christian Church. One went up to Jerusalem since it was sited at an altitude of 2,400 feet above sea level.

**apostles.** A key qualification in being an apostle was to have seen the resurrected Jesus (1 Cor. 9:1).

**before I was.** The only distinction Paul admits between his apostleship and that of the leaders in Jerusalem is that of time. They were commissioned by Jesus earlier than he was.

**Arabia.** The desert-like region to the east of Damascus was part of Arabia. In the tradition of Old Testament prophets (and of Jesus after his baptism), Paul retreats into the desert for solitude and reflection. He probably also preached to the Gentiles there, both in the cities and to the wandering Bedouins. That he was actively at work in Arabia can be inferred from 2 Corinthians 11:32–33 where it appears that he had somehow offended King Aretas, the ruler of Arabia, who sent representatives into Damascus to arrest him.

**1:18–19** "Paul's first visit to Jerusalem was only after three years, it lasted only two weeks, and he saw only two apostles. It was, therefore, ludicrous to suggest that he obtained his gospel from the Jerusalem apostles" (Stott).

**1:18 after three years.** A significant interval of time elapsed between his conversion and his first visit to Jerusalem, i.e., he had already begun his ministry to the Gentiles prior to any authorization by the leaders in Jerusalem.

**Jerusalem.** It was a courageous act by Paul to return here—to his former friends who might well try to harm him (because of his conversion to Christianity), and to new friends who might not even receive him (because of their suspicions about him).

**to get acquainted.** It was important that Paul come to know the leaders of the church, in particular Peter (who was its undisputed head). They, in turn, needed to hear a first-hand account of his conversion.

**fifteen days.** This was a short visit and certainly not a time when Paul's apostleship was upgraded and confirmed as a result of in-depth apostolic instruction. In fact, Paul spent much of his time preaching (Acts 9:28–29).

**1:19 James.** See Mark 6:3; Acts 1:13. James eventually became the leader of the Jerusalem church. He was a strict and orthodox Jew.

**1:20 I assure you.** The taking of oaths was discouraged unless absolutely necessary (which Paul considers this to be, as he defends the independence of this Gospel and the validity of his apostleship).

**1:21 Syria and Cilicia.** After leaving Jerusalem Paul went north into Syria and then into the adjacent area of Cilicia to the city of Tarsus, his birthplace. At the time both regions were joined together into a single Roman province. Paul continues to assert his independence by pointing out that soon after this quick visit to Jerusalem, he left the area.

**1:22 personally unknown.** If Paul had been controlled by the Jewish Christians in Jerusalem, Judea would probably have been where he was sent to do missionary work. But as it was, the churches in Judea had only heard reports of him (v. 23).

**1:24** Even though the Judaizers in Galatia might be critical of Paul, the Christians in Judea praised God because of him.

6·13· 2001

## THREE-PART AGENDA

**ICE-BREAKER**
15 Minutes

**BIBLE STUDY**
30 Minutes

**CARING TIME**
15–45 Minutes

> *LEADER: If there's a new person in this session, start with an ice-breaker from the center section (see page M7). Remember to stick closely to the three-part agenda and the time allowed for each segment. Is your group praying for the empty chair?*

## TO BEGIN THE BIBLE STUDY TIME
(Choose 1 or 2)

1. What kind of races have you been in: Athletic? Motorcycle or Car? Political? The "rat race"? Other?

2. What do you work on the most about your appearance?

3. What did you feel peer pressure to do as a teenager?

## READ SCRIPTURE & DISCUSS
(If you don't have time for all the questions in this section, conclude the Bible Study [30 min.] by answering question #7.)

1. When have you worked hard on something, only to have it turn out to be in vain?

2. Why was Paul concerned that his preaching to the Gentiles was "in vain" (see last note on v. 2)?

3. Who were the "false brothers" (v. 4)? What were they doing to Paul and his ministry? With what results?

4. What response did Paul get from the disciples in Jerusalem?

## Paul Accepted by the Apostles

**2** *Fourteen years later I went up again to Jerusalem, this time with Barnabas. I took Titus along also. ²I went in response to a revelation and set before them the gospel that I preach among the Gentiles. But I did this privately to those who seemed to be leaders, for fear that I was running or had run my race in vain. ³Yet not even Titus, who was with me, was compelled to be circumcised, even though he was a Greek. ⁴This matter arose because some false brothers had infiltrated our ranks to spy on the freedom we have in Christ Jesus and to make us slaves. ⁵We did not give in to them for a moment, so that the truth of the gospel might remain with you.*

*⁶As for those who seemed to be important—whatever they were makes no difference to me; God does not judge by external appearance—those men added nothing to my message. ⁷On the contrary, they saw that I had been entrusted with the task of preaching the gospel to the Gentiles,ᵃ just as Peter had been to the Jews.ᵇ ⁸For God, who was at work in the ministry of Peter as an apostle to the Jews, was also at work in my ministry as an apostle to the Gentiles. ⁹James, Peterᶜ and John, those reputed to be pillars, gave me and Barnabas the right hand of fellowship when they recognized the grace given to me. They agreed that we should go to the Gentiles, and they to the Jews. ¹⁰All they asked was that we should continue to remember the poor, the very thing I was eager to do.*

ᵃ7 Greek *uncircumcised*  ᵇ7 Greek *circumcised;* also in verses 8 and 9
ᶜ9 Greek *Cephas;* also in verses 11 and 14

5. How would you have felt about Paul joining your group, knowing he had persecuted the church?

6. How do you handle pressure to change your beliefs?

7. What can you and this group do to "remember the poor"?

## CARING TIME

(Choose 1 or 2 of these questions before closing in prayer. Be sure to pray for the empty chair.)

1. How would you describe your relationship with God right now: Close? Distant? Improving? Strained? Other?

2. How are you doing at inviting others to the group? Who could you invite for next week?

3. How can the group support you in prayer this week?

**2:1 *Fourteen years later.*** It is not clear whether Paul means 14 years after his conversion or after his first visit to Jerusalem. In any case, the significant factor is that Paul had little contact with the leaders in Jerusalem. He was not their missionary. He did not take orders from them.

***I went up again.*** In 14 years Paul made only two fleeting visits to Jerusalem. The first was for the purpose of meeting Peter. The second was necessary in order to deliver to the mother church a famine collection donated by Christians at Antioch.

***Barnabas.*** A Levite from Cyprus, whose name was actually Joseph but who had been nicknamed Barnabas (Son of Encouragement) by the apostles, presumably because he was that sort of person (Acts 4:36). When the church in Jerusalem heard that a great number of people in Antioch had turned to Jesus, they sent Barnabas to verify what was happening. Barnabas in turn, having seen this to be an authentic work of God, sought out Paul in Tarsus and brought him back to Antioch, where the two of them labored together to establish the church (Acts 11:19-30).

> Paul preached that Gentiles could become Christians without first becoming Jews, i.e., that there was one church made up of both Jews and Gentiles.

***Titus.*** A Gentile Christian from Antioch. Titus became an important coworker with Paul (2 Cor. 2:12–13; 7:13–16; 8:6–24; 12:18) and later was the recipient of a Pastoral Letter.

**2:2 *in response to a revelation.*** Paul makes it quite clear that it was God who told him to visit Jerusalem. It was not a matter of the leaders there calling him to account for his actions.

***privately.*** Perhaps Paul hoped for a more understanding response than might be possible were this issue to be aired openly in front of the whole church.

***in vain.*** Paul preached that Gentiles could become Christians without first becoming Jews, i.e., that there was one church made up of both Jews and Gentiles. If the leaders in Jerusalem disputed this, his 14 years of work would have been in vain. "A cleavage between his Gentile mission and the mother church would be disastrous: Christ would be divided, and all the energy which Paul had devoted, and hoped to devote, to the evangelizing of the Gentile world would be frustrated" (Bruce).

**2:3** This did not happen. Even Titus (an uncircumcised Gentile Christian) was accepted—fully—right in the heart of Jewish Christianity.

**2:4** The need for this discussion arose because some Jewish Christians disputed the idea that Gentiles need not observe the Jewish laws to be fully Christian.

***to spy.*** With the intention of bringing such freedom to an end.

***freedom.*** Jew and Gentile Christians freely mixed, eating together and having fellowship. This stood in stark contrast to the way Jews and Gentiles normally related.

**2:5 *did not give in.*** On another occasion, Paul did have Timothy circumcised "because of the Jews who lived in that area" (Acts 16:3), but Timothy's mother was Jewish and Paul never suggested that Jews not be circumcised.

**2:6 *As for those.*** Paul resumes the main thread of his argument (vv. 3–5 having been a parenthesis).

***who seemed to be important.*** This phrase (as well as those in v. 2—"seemed to be leaders," and v. 9—"reputed to be pillars") might be construed to imply disrespect on Paul's part. In fact, Paul intended nothing of the sort. These men were authentic leaders and well-respected. What might have concerned Paul is that some of the Judaizers were exalting the role and position of these men (while they downplayed his own).

***makes no difference to me.*** The difference between these men and Paul is that they were founding members of the church and he was a late-comer. Still, each of them received his commission directly from the Lord.

**God does not judge by external appearance.** "God does not favor companions or relatives of the historical Jesus over someone, like Paul, who received his apostolic commission later" (Bruce).

**added nothing.** "No question was raised, apparently, about the comparative contents of Paul's gospel and theirs, any more than the question was raised about Paul's authority to preach his gospel. His gospel was unexceptionable; his commission was undisputed: the agenda, we gather, concentrated on the demarcation of the respective spheres of service of the parties to the discussion" (Bruce).

**2:7 On the contrary.** In fact, they acknowledged his sphere of authority.

**to the Gentiles.** Though Paul did on occasions evangelize Jews (Acts 9:20; 26:20) his major mission was to the Gentiles (Acts 22:21).

**to the Jews.** Though on one occasion Peter evangelized Gentiles such as in the home of Cornelius (Acts 10:1–11:18; 15:7–9), this was the exception, not the rule. God used that particular occasion to teach Peter (and through him, the church at Jerusalem) that he was doing a new and unexpected thing: God was calling Gentiles to be his people. Peter's mission—which he carried out with great effectiveness—was to reach his own people in Jerusalem and Judea (Acts 2:14–41; 3:11–26; 9:32).

**2:8** Both ministries were confirmed by God with signs and wonders as well as with fruit.

**2:9 James.** On his first visit to Jerusalem, Peter was clearly the leader of the mother church. However, after his escape from Herod Agrippa's prison (Acts 12:17) Peter left Jerusalem. Though he did return, increasingly the ministry of he and other members of the Twelve took them away from Jerusalem—leaving James, the brother of Jesus, as the leader of the mother church. It is clear that even Peter followed James' directions (2:12).

**John.** The son of Zebedee.

**2:10 remember the poor.** In fact, this is why Paul and Barnabas had come to Jerusalem—to deliver an offering given by the Christians at Antioch. In later years, Paul continued to raise funds for relief in Jerusalem (Rom. 15:25–28; 1 Cor. 16:1–4; 2 Cor. 8:1–9:15).

# 5 Paul Opposes Peter—Gal. 2:11–21

6/20/2001

## THREE-PART AGENDA

**ICE-BREAKER**
15 Minutes

**BIBLE STUDY**
30 Minutes

**CARING TIME**
15–45 Minutes

**LEADER:** *If there's a new person in this session, start with an ice-breaker from the center section (see page M7). Remember to stick closely to the three-part agenda and the time allowed for each segment. Is your group praying for the empty chair? As the leader, you may want to choose question #1 in the Caring Time to facilitate the group in handling accountability issues.*

## TO BEGIN THE BIBLE STUDY TIME
(Choose 1 or 2)

1. What family custom do you look forward to each year?

2. What traffic law do you have the most trouble obeying?

3. Growing up, when did a "friend" lead you astray and get you into trouble?

## READ SCRIPTURE & DISCUSS
(If you don't have time for all the questions in this section, conclude the Bible Study [30 min.] by answering question #7.)

1. What's the last big disagreement you had with a family member or friend? How did it turn out?

2. What disagreement did Paul have with Peter? Why was Peter afraid (see first note on v. 12)?

3. Why was Paul so adamant about Gentiles not having to follow Jewish customs?

Paul Opposes Peter

*[11] When Peter came to Antioch, I opposed him to his face, because he was clearly in the wrong. [12] Before certain men came from James, he used to eat with the Gentiles. But when they arrived, he began to draw back and separate himself from the Gentiles because he was afraid of those who belonged to the circumcision group. [13] The other Jews joined him in his hypocrisy, so that by their hypocrisy even Barnabas was led astray.*

*[14] When I saw that they were not acting in line with the truth of the gospel, I said to Peter in front of them all, "You are a Jew, yet you live like a Gentile and not like a Jew. How is it, then, that you force Gentiles to follow Jewish customs?*

*[15] "We who are Jews by birth and not 'Gentile sinners' [16] know that a man is not justified by observing the law, but by faith in Jesus Christ. So we, too, have put our faith in Christ Jesus that we may be justified by faith in Christ and not by observing the law, because by observing the law no one will be justified.*

*[17] "If, while we seek to be justified in Christ, it becomes evident that we ourselves are sinners, does that mean that Christ promotes sin? Absolutely not! [18] If I rebuild what I destroyed, I prove that I am a lawbreaker. [19] For through the law I died to the law so that I might live for God. [20] I have been crucified with Christ and I no longer live, but Christ lives in me. The life I live in the body, I live by faith in the Son of God, who loved me and gave himself for me. [21] I do not set aside the grace of God, for if righteousness could be gained through the law, Christ died for nothing!"* [a]

[a] 21 Some interpreters end the quotation after verse 14.

4. How would the church be different today if Paul had ignored this situation?

5. What does the concept of justification mean (see second note on v. 16)? How is a person "justified in Christ" (v. 17)?

6. Applying the principle of verse 20, who is "alive" in your life right now—"I," or "Christ in me"?

7. How is God's grace evident in this passage? In what situation do you especially need the "grace of God" in the coming week?

## CARING TIME

(Choose 1 or 2 of these questions before closing in prayer. Be sure to pray for the empty chair.)

1. For what would you like this group to help hold you accountable?

2. What is something for which you are particularly thankful?

3. How can the group remember you in prayer this week?

**2:11–14** Paul concludes his autobiographical sketch by recounting an incident in which he had to rebuke Peter for his inconsistency. This showed beyond a shadow of a doubt that Paul was not under the jurisdiction of the Jerusalem leaders. This incident most likely occurred after Paul's return to Antioch from his second visit to Jerusalem (2:1–10), but prior to his first missionary journey (Acts 13–14) during which he founded the Galatian churches (though it is also possible that vv. 11–14 occurred after the mission to Cyprus and South Galatia).

**2:11 *in the wrong.*** Literally, condemned, not because of overt law-breaking but by the inconsistency of his behavior.

**2:12 *from James.*** Though he eventually sided with Paul and the others in agreeing that Gentiles need not be bound by Jewish customs (Acts 15), James is clearly quite conservative on this issue. Perhaps he was warning the Jewish Christians in Antioch that their liberty was giving deep offense to the more conservative brothers back in Jerusalem; or that their behavior was hindering the evangelization of the Jews in general. Perhaps he even warned, in the light of newly revived Jewish militancy, that such actions were dangerous and could result in Jewish Christians being branded traitors by the militants. This latter view is strengthened by the fact that Peter was afraid. The reference to the circumcision party may be to these militants (Bruce).

***he used to eat.*** Eating together was a sign of fellowship and indeed strong evidence that Christians—regardless of racial identity—had been made one family, having acknowledged one Lord and shared in one baptism and in one communion table (Eph. 2:11–3:13). Peter's action in eating with Gentiles is consistent with his behavior after his vision at Joppa (Acts 10)—he was quite willing to visit Cornelius and eat with his family (Acts 10:28; 11:3). "If Gentile Christians were not fit company for Jewish Christians, it must be because their Christianity was defective: faith in Christ and baptism into his name were insufficient and must be supplemented with something else. And that 'something else' could only be a measure of conformity to Jewish law or custom: they must, in other words, Judaize" (Bruce).

***with the Gentiles.*** Though not strictly forbidden by the Law of Moses, at this point in history Jews simply did not eat with Gentiles, lest they consume "unclean" food or eat with contaminated utensils, and so become ritually impure.

**2:13 *hypocrisy.*** Literally, play acting, a word derived from the Greek stage where it was used to describe actors who hid their true selves behind the role they were playing. Hence, it came to mean doing something one does not really believe in.

***even Barnabas.*** This must have been the hardest blow of all for Paul—to see his close associate in the Gentile mission capitulate to the circumcision party.

> *Jews did rather arrogantly look down on all Gentiles. But Paul's point is that both Jew and Gentile come to God by faith not by works. Being "better" morally has nothing to do with justification.*

**2:14 *in line with.*** Literally, to be on the right road. Paul felt they were turning in a new direction by such hypocrisy.

***in front of them all.*** The issue was public and thus had to be confronted in an open forum. Paul probably knew where Peter's heart was and so risked such a confrontation because he was confident that he and Peter shared the same view of the Gospel.

***live like a Gentile.*** By disregarding Jewish prohibitions.

***force Gentiles.*** The logic is impeccable. By what reasoning could a Jew (who felt free to disregard the rules and regulations himself) demand that a Gentile be bound by what he, the Jew, had forsaken?!

**2:15–21** Paul now leaves his own story and moves into the core of his theological case. Here he states the crux of his argument. In chapters 3–4 he will expound, extend and explain the universal principle set down here.

**2:15** *"Gentile sinners."* There was a great moral guilt in the first century between Jewish and Gentile communities (despite exceptions in both directions). Even pagan writers decried the depravity of certain Gentiles. Still, Jews did rather arrogantly look down on all Gentiles. But Paul's point is that both Jew and Gentile come to God by faith not by works. Being "better" morally has nothing to do with justification.

**2:16** The key verse in Galatians in which the two options are clearly delineated by Paul whereby people might think to obtain right standing before God: by their own activity in law-keeping, or by simple trust in Jesus. In fact, there is only one path to right standing, namely, faith in Christ.

*justified.* Behind this word stands the image of the Judgment Day. The Jew was preoccupied with how one obtained a positive verdict (justification) from God the Judge, with how one gained "right standing" before God. The opposite of justification is condemnation—to be declared guilty—on Judgment Day. Within this concept one also finds the ideas of reconciliation, forgiveness, and restoration.

*observing the law.* The Law is the sum of God's commandments. The Jews supposed that by keeping the Law, they could obtain right standing (justification) before God.

*by faith.* Right standing before God is made possible because of the death of Christ (not the *work* of any individual person), and the benefits of his death are appropriated simply by faith.

*in Jesus Christ.* It is not *faith* in general that saves, but *faith in* a particular person. The person who has faith in *Jesus Christ* is the person who accepts that in the life, death and resurrection of Jesus Christ one sees the power of God at work. That person then responds to God by submitting to Jesus Christ and trusting in God's powerful work to save them.

**2:17** Verses 17–18 are difficult to understand. Paul may mean that when law-abiding Jews like he and Peter turn to Christ for justification, they de facto become like the Gentile sinners (v. 15).

*Christ promotes sin.* In the sense that now all those law-abiding Jews are shown, in fact, to be *sinners,* and so the sheer number of sinners increases.

**2:18** If anyone who received justification by faith in Christ submits to circumcision (i.e., reinstates the Law in place of Christ), that person makes themselves a sinner all over again—and Christ is not responsible for that.

**2:19** Paul seems to be saying that he cannot be a lawbreaker because he has died in relationship to the Law. He no longer lives in the sphere where the Law is operative (i.e., Judaism). Rather he has a new Lord, Jesus, for whom he now lives.

**2:20** *I have been crucified with Christ.* On the Damascus road when Christ met him, "the old Paul died—not only the cruel little persecutor of the Christians, hating himself for it as we may surmise, but also the virtuous Pharisee who knew that his virtue was a hollow pretense, the godly rabbi who knew that his inner life was a travesty of what he professed in public" (Neil).

*I no longer live.* Paul died in relationship to the Law.

*Christ lives in me.* That which now activates the believer is the resurrection life and power of Jesus.

*I live by faith.* Faith is that which bonds together the believer and the risen Christ. Paul will also refer to this as *living by the Spirit* (5:25).

**2:21** *set aside the grace of God.* This was the error of the Judaizers.

*righteousness.* In Hebrew thought, righteousness is not so much a moral quality as it is a legal judgment. The idea here is not that a person is made righteous (in the ethical sense) or proved to be righteous (i.e., virtuous) as a result of having trusted Jesus. Rather, that person is counted or reckoned as righteous (even though they are really guilty). They are *pardoned.* They are given right standing before God, by *grace* operating through the death of Christ.

*Christ died for nothing.* This is the conclusion of his argument against the Judaizers. If they were right, Christ died for nothing.

# 6 Faith or the Law—Gal. 3:1-14

## THREE-PART AGENDA

**ICE-BREAKER**
15 Minutes

**BIBLE STUDY**
30 Minutes

**CARING TIME**
15–45 Minutes

> *LEADER: Check page M7 in the center section for a good ice-breaker, particularly if you have a new person at this meeting. Is your group working well together—with everyone "fielding their position" as shown on the team roster on page M5?*

## TO BEGIN THE BIBLE STUDY TIME
(Choose 1 or 2)

1. Who helped you to stay on the "straight and narrow path" when you were a teenager?

2. Who is your favorite Old Testament character?

3. When have you received news that seemed too good to be true?

## READ SCRIPTURE & DISCUSS
(If you don't have time for all the questions in this section, conclude the Bible Study [30 min.] by answering question #7.)

1. How do you usually handle advice from family and friends?

2. What question does Paul ask the Galatians in verse 2? Why is this issue so crucial?

3. How does a person receive the Spirit (see notes on v. 2)? What "goal" (v. 3) does the Spirit help a person to achieve that human effort cannot attain?

4. What does the example of Abraham teach us about faith and righteousness?

## Faith or Observance of the Law

**3** *You foolish Galatians! Who has bewitched you? Before your very eyes Jesus Christ was clearly portrayed as crucified. ²I would like to learn just one thing from you: Did you receive the Spirit by observing the law, or by believing what you heard? ³Are you so foolish? After beginning with the Spirit, are you now trying to attain your goal by human effort? ⁴Have you suffered so much for nothing—if it really was for nothing? ⁵Does God give you his Spirit and work miracles among you because you observe the law, or because you believe what you heard?*

*⁶Consider Abraham: "He believed God, and it was credited to him as righteousness."*ᵃ *⁷Understand, then, that those who believe are children of Abraham. ⁸The Scripture foresaw that God would justify the Gentiles by faith, and announced the gospel in advance to Abraham: "All nations will be blessed through you."*ᵇ *⁹So those who have faith are blessed along with Abraham, the man of faith.*

*¹⁰All who rely on observing the law are under a curse, for it is written: "Cursed is everyone who does not continue to do everything written in the Book of the Law."*ᶜ *¹¹Clearly no one is justified before God by the law, because, "The righteous will live by faith."*ᵈ *¹²The law is not based on faith; on the contrary, "The man who does these things will live by them."*ᵉ *¹³Christ redeemed us from the curse of the law by becoming a curse for us, for it is written: "Cursed is everyone who is hung on a tree."*ᶠ *¹⁴He redeemed us in order that the blessing given to Abraham might come to the Gentiles through Christ Jesus, so that by faith we might receive the promise of the Spirit.*

ᵃ*6* Gen. 15:6   ᵇ*8* Gen. 12:3; 18:18; 22:18   ᶜ*10* Deut. 27:26
ᵈ*11* Hab. 2:4   ᵉ*12* Lev. 18:5   ᶠ*13* Deut. 21:23

5. What kind of balance should there be between "observing the law" (v. 2) and faith?

6. Lately, have you been feeling more blessed or cursed? How can verses 13 and 14 help you?

7. How can you walk more fully in the blessings of the Spirit available to the children of Abraham?

## CARING TIME

(Choose 1 or 2 of these questions before closing in prayer. Be sure to pray for the empty chair.)

1. How is the group doing with its "team assignments" (review the team roster on p. M5)?

2. Rate this past week on a scale of 1 (terrible) to 10 (great). What's the outlook for this week?

3. How would you like the group to pray for you this week?

**3:1–5** Paul challenges the Galatians to consider whether the work of the Spirit among them came by the Law or by faith. His point is that if (as they know) the gift of the Spirit was by faith, to return to law-keeping is just plain stupid!

**3:1 foolish.** Paul's feelings of exasperation and indignation flare up. How could they have been so *stupid* (as the NEB translates the word)? It is not that they were unable to understand what was happening. They simply failed to use their minds.

**bewitched.** Black magic was rife in Galatia. Paul is saying that they act as if the Judaizers had put a spell on them. Their behavior was so unexpected it was almost as if they had been hypnotized.

**3:2** Paul asks them to recall that their conversion experience had nothing to do with observing the Law. The gift of the Spirit—assumed to be the most significant experience a person can have—came by faith. Once this is noted, nothing further need be said about the inadequacy of law-keeping.

**I would like to learn just one thing.** If they concede this, Paul's whole argument must be accepted and believed.

**receive the Spirit.** Faith in Christ brings both justification (2:16) and the gift of the Spirit.

**3:3** Could they actually believe that spiritual life had anything to do with the observance of human customs and laws?

**foolish.** Their immature return to legalistic obedience to the Law (when they know by what means they received the Spirit) justifies Paul's use of this strong adjective.

**3:4 suffered.** We are never told about the nature of their persecution, but the implication here is that they had suffered for their faith (all of which would have been pointless if they could have received salvation simply by circumcision and law-keeping). Why then suffer as a result of following the crucified Christ?

**3:5 miracles.** Extraordinary things happened in the early Christian church: lives were changed, people were healed (Acts 14:8–10), demons were cast out, some (like Dorcas) were even restored to life (Acts 9:32–43). The Galatians actually experienced the power of the Holy Spirit. All this stood in sharp contrast to their experiences as pagan idol-worshipers.

**3:6-9** Paul turns from his argument based on their experience to an argument based on Old Testament Scripture. Here he shows that it has always been by faith that men and women became God's children.

**3:6 He believed God.** God promised Abraham descendants as numerous as the stars, even though his wife Sarah was barren! Despite the improbability of this ever happening, Abraham still trusted God that it would be so. Paul does not argue here, as he does in Romans 4:10–12, that such faith came prior to circumcision and thus had nothing to do with works, probably because his Gentile audience was also uncircumcised and so might respond: "Well then, now that we have faith we too like Abraham need circumcision next!"

**credited ... as righteousness.** For Abraham, right standing before God came by faith, not by law-keeping in general (or circumcision in particular).

**3:7 children of Abraham.** The real sons and daughters of Abraham are not those who are his racial descendants, but those who believe—be they Jew or Gentile.

**3:8 announced the gospel in advance.** The promise to Abraham foreshadowed the Gospel and is only fulfilled in the Gospel. This is how Paul can use passages from Genesis to prove his point: there is continuity between Abraham's faith and the faith of Christians (John 8:56).

**3:9 blessed.** Not only are people of faith sons and daughters of Abraham, but they also share in the blessings which were promised to Abraham.

> *The gift of the Spirit—assumed to be the most significant experience a person can have—came by faith.*

# Leadership Training Supplement

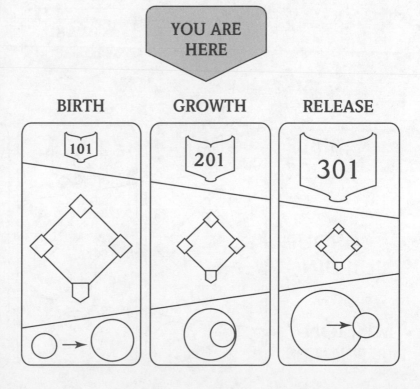

YOU ARE HERE

| BIRTH | GROWTH | RELEASE |
| --- | --- | --- |
| 101 | 201 | 301 |

# What is the game plan for your group in the 201 stage?

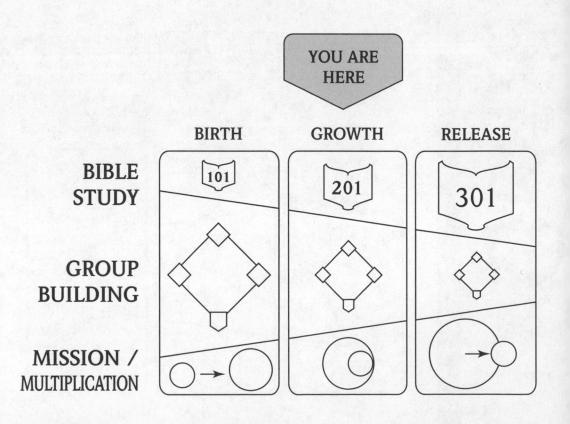

YOU ARE HERE

| | BIRTH | GROWTH | RELEASE |
|---|---|---|---|
| BIBLE STUDY | 101 | 201 | 301 |
| GROUP BUILDING | | | |
| MISSION / MULTIPLICATION | | | |

The three essentials in a healthy small group are Bible Study, Group Building and Mission / Multiplication. You need all three to stay balanced—like a 3-legged stool.
- To focus only on Bible Study will lead to scholasticism.
- To focus only on Group Building will lead to narcissism.
- To focus only on Mission will lead to burnout.

You need a game plan for the life cycle of the group where all of these elements are present in a purpose-driven strategy:

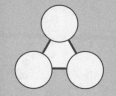

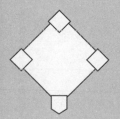

**The 3-Legged Stool**

# Bible Study

**To dig into Scripture as a group.**

Group Bible Study is quite different from individual Bible Study. The guided discussion questions are open-ended. And for those with little Bible background, there are reference notes to bring this person up to speed.

# Group Building

**To transform your group into a mission-driven team.**

The nine basic needs of a group will be assigned to nine different people. Everyone has a job to fill, and when everyone is doing their job the group will grow spiritually and numerically. When new people enter the group, there is a selection of ICE-BREAKERS to start off the meeting and let the new people get acquainted.

# Mission / Multiplication

**To identify the Apprentice / Leader for birthing a new group.**

In this stage, you will start dreaming about the possibility of starting a new group down the road. The questions at the close of each session will lead you carefully through the dreaming process—to help you discover an Apprentice / Leader who will eventually be the leader of a new group. This is an exciting challenge! (See page M6 for more about Mission / Multiplication.)

## Bible Study

**What is unique about Serendipity Group Bible Study?**

Bible Study for groups is based on six principles. Principle 1: Level the playing field so that everyone can share—those who know the Bible and those who do not know the Bible. Principle 2: Share your spiritual story and let the people in your group get to know you. Principle 3: Ask open-ended questions that have no right or wrong answers. Principle 4: Keep a tight agenda. Principle 5: Subdivide into smaller groups so that everyone can participate. Principle 6: Affirm One Another—"Thanks for sharing."

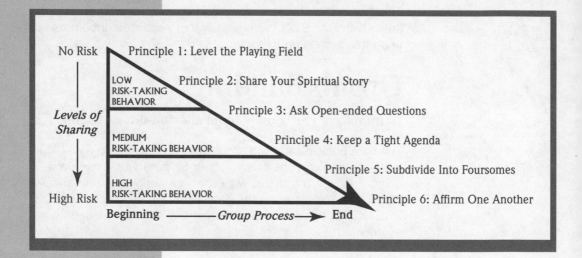

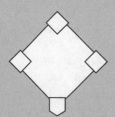

## Group Building

**What are the jobs that are needed on your team roster?**

In the first or second session of this course, you need to fill out the roster on the next page. Then check every few weeks to see that everyone is "playing their position." If you do not have nine people in your group, you can double up on jobs until new people join your group and are assigned a job.

# Your Small Group Team Roster

**Mission Leader**
(Left Field)
Keeps group focused on the mission to invite new people and eventually give birth to a new group. This person needs to be passionate and have a long-term perspective.

_____

**Host**
(Center Field)
Environmental engineer in charge of meeting location. Always on the lookout for moving to a new meeting location where new people will feel the "home field advantage."

_____

**Social Leader**
(Right Field)
Designates who is going to bring refreshments. Plans a party every month or so where new people are invited to visit and children are welcome.

_____

**Caretaker**
(Shortstop)
Takes new members under their wing. Makes sure they get acquainted. Always has an extra book, name tags and a list of group members and phone numbers.

_____

**Bible Study Leader**
(Second Base)
Takes over in the Bible Study time (30 minutes). Follows the agenda. Keeps the group moving. This person must be very time-conscious.

_____

**Group Leader**
(Pitcher)
Puts ball in play. Team encourager. Motivator. Sees to it that everyone is involved in the team effort.

_____

**Caring Time Leader**
(Third Base)
Takes over in the Caring Time. Records prayer requests and follows up on any prayer needs during the week. This person is the "heart" of the group.

_____

**Worship Leader**
(First Base)
Starts the meeting with singing and prayer. If a new person comes, shifts immediately to an ice-breaker to get acquainted, before the opening prayer.

_____

**Apprentice / Leader**
(Catcher)
The other half of the battery. Observes the infield. Calls "time" to discuss strategy and regroup. Stays focused.

_____

# Mission / Multiplication

**Where are you in the 3-stage life cycle of your mission?**

You can't sit on a one-legged stool—or even a two-legged stool. It takes all three. The same is true of a small group; you need all three legs. A Bible Study and Care Group will eventually fall if it does not have a mission.

The mission goal is to eventually give birth to a new group. In this 201 course, the goals are: 1) to keep inviting new people to join your group and 2) to discover the Apprentice / Leader and leadership core for starting a new group down the road.

When a new person comes to the group, start off the meeting with one of the ice-breakers on the following pages. These ice-breakers are designed to be fun and easy to share, but they have a very important purpose—that is, to let the new person get acquainted with the group and share their spiritual story with the group, and hear the spiritual stories of those in the group.

YOU ARE
HERE

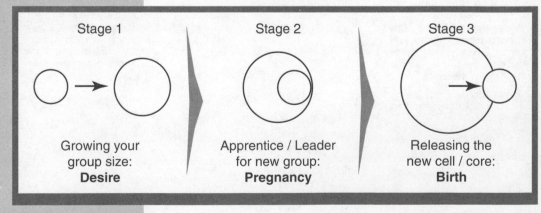

| Stage 1 | Stage 2 | Stage 3 |
|---|---|---|
| Growing your group size: **Desire** | Apprentice / Leader for new group: **Pregnancy** | Releasing the new cell / core: **Birth** |

# Ice-Breakers

# I Am Somebody Who ...

Rotate around the group, one person reading the first item, the next person reading the second item, etc. Before answering, let everyone in the group try to GUESS what the answer would be: "Yes" ... "No" ... or "Maybe." After everyone has guessed, explain the answer. Anyone who guessed right gets $10. When every item on the list has been read, the person with the most "money" WINS.

I AM SOMEBODY WHO ...

**Y N M**
- ❏ ❏ ❏ would go on a blind date
- ❏ ❏ ❏ sings in the shower
- ❏ ❏ ❏ listens to music full blast
- ❏ ❏ ❏ likes to dance
- ❏ ❏ ❏ cries at movies
- ❏ ❏ ❏ stops to smell the flowers
- ❏ ❏ ❏ daydreams a lot
- ❏ ❏ ❏ likes to play practical jokes
- ❏ ❏ ❏ makes a "to do" list
- ❏ ❏ ❏ loves liver
- ❏ ❏ ❏ won't use a portable toilet
- ❏ ❏ ❏ likes thunderstorms
- ❏ ❏ ❏ enjoys romance novels
- ❏ ❏ ❏ loves crossword puzzles
- ❏ ❏ ❏ hates flying
- ❏ ❏ ❏ fixes my own car

**Y N M**
- ❏ ❏ ❏ would enjoy skydiving
- ❏ ❏ ❏ has a black belt in karate
- ❏ ❏ ❏ watches soap operas
- ❏ ❏ ❏ is afraid of the dark
- ❏ ❏ ❏ goes to bed early
- ❏ ❏ ❏ plays the guitar
- ❏ ❏ ❏ talks to plants
- ❏ ❏ ❏ will ask a stranger for directions
- ❏ ❏ ❏ sleeps until the last second
- ❏ ❏ ❏ likes to travel alone
- ❏ ❏ ❏ reads the financial page
- ❏ ❏ ❏ saves for a rainy day
- ❏ ❏ ❏ lies about my age
- ❏ ❏ ❏ yells at the umpire
- ❏ ❏ ❏ closes my eyes during scary movies

# Press Conference

This is a great activity for a new group or when new people are joining an established group. Interview one person with these questions.

1. What is your nickname and how did you get it?

2. Where did you grow up? Where was the "watering hole" in your home-town—where kids got together?

3. What did you do for kicks then? What about now?

4. What was the turning point in your spiritual life?

5. What prompted you to come to this group?

6. What do you want to get out of this group?

# Down Memory Lane

Celebrate the childhood memories of the way you were. Choose one or more of the topics listed below and take turns answering the question related to it. If time allows, do another round.

HOME SWEET HOME–What do you remember about your childhood home?

TELEVISION—What was your favorite TV program or radio show?

OLD SCHOOLHOUSE—What were your best and worst subjects in school?

LIBRARY—What did you like to read (and where)?

TELEPHONE—How much time did you spend on the phone each day?

MOVIES—Who was your favorite movie star?

CASH FLOW—What did you do for spending money?

SPORTS—What was your favorite sport or team?

GRANDPA'S HOUSE—Where did your grandparents live? When did you visit them?

POLICE—Did you ever get in trouble with the law?

WEEKENDS—What was the thing to do on Saturday night?

# Wallet Scavenger Hunt

With your wallet or purse, use the set of questions below. You get two minutes in silence to go through your possessions and find these items. Then break the silence and "show-and-tell" what you have chosen. For instance, "The thing I have had for the longest time is ... this picture of me when I was a baby."

1.  The thing I have had for the LONGEST TIME in my wallet is ...

2.  The thing that has SENTIMENTAL VALUE is ...

3.  The thing that reminds me of a FUN TIME is ...

4.  The most REVEALING thing about me in my wallet is ...

# The Grand Total

This is a fun ice-breaker that has additional uses. You can use this ice-breaker to divide your group into two subgroups (odds and evens). You can also calculate who has the highest and lowest totals if you need a fun way to select someone to do a particular task, such as bring refreshments or be first to tell their story.

Fill each box with the correct number and then total your score. When everyone is finished, go around the group and explain how you got your total.

|  |  |  |
|---|---|---|
| ☐ X | ☐ = | ☐ |
| Number of hours you sleep | Number of miles you walk daily | Subtotal |

|  |  |  |
|---|---|---|
| ☐ — | ☐ = | ☐ |
| Number of speeding tickets you've received | Number of times sent to principal's office | Subtotal |

|  |  |  |
|---|---|---|
| ☐ ÷ | ☐ = | ☐ |
| Number of hours spent watching TV daily | Number of books you read this year for fun | Subtotal |

|  |  |  |
|---|---|---|
| ☐ + | ☐ = | ☐ |
| Number of push-ups you can do | Number of pounds you lost this year | Subtotal |

☐

GRAND TOTAL

# Find Yourself in the Picture

In this drawing, which child do you identify with—or which one best portrays you right now? Share with your group which child you would choose and why. You can also use this as an affirmation exercise, by assigning each person in your group to a child in the picture.

# Four Facts, One Lie

Everyone in the group should answer the following five questions. One of the five answers should be a lie! The rest of the group members can guess which of your answers is a lie.

1. At age 7, my favorite TV show was ...

2. At age 9, my hero was ...

3. At age 11, I wanted to be a ...

4. At age 13, my favorite music was ...

5. Right now, my favorite pastime is ...

# Old-Fashioned Auction

Just like an old-fashioned auction, conduct an out loud auction in your group—starting each item at $50. Everybody starts out with $1,000. Select an auctioneer. This person can also get in on the bidding. Remember, start the bidding on each item at $50. Then, write the winning bid in the left column and the winner's name in the right column. Remember, you only have $1,000 to spend for the whole game. AUCTIONEER: Start off by asking, "Who will give me $50 for a 1965 red MG convertible?" ... and keep going until you have a winner. Keep this auction to 10 minutes.

WINNING BID                                                        WINNER

$_____ 1965 red MG convertible in perfect condition      _____

$_____ Winter vacation in Hawaii for two                 _____

$_____ Two Super Bowl tickets on the 50-yard line        _____

$_____ One year of no hassles with my kids / parents     _____

$_____ Holy Land tour hosted by my favorite Christian    _____
                leader

$_____ Season pass to ski resort of my choice            _____

$_____ Two months off to do anything I want, with pay    _____

$_____ Home theater with surround sound                  _____

$_____ Breakfast in bed for one year                     _____

$_____ Two front-row tickets at the concert of my choice _____

$_____ Two-week Caribbean cruise with my spouse in        _____
                honeymoon suite

$_____ Shopping spree at Saks Fifth Avenue               _____

$_____ Six months of maid service                        _____

$_____ All-expense-paid family vacation to Disney World_____

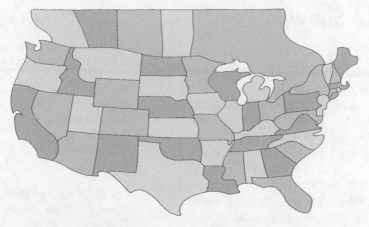

# Places in My Life

On the map above, put six dots to indicate these significant places in your journey. Then go around and have each person explain the dots:

• the place where I was born

• the place where I spent most of my life

• the place where I first fell in love

• the place where I went or would like to go on a honeymoon

• the place where God first became real to me

• the place where I would like to retire

# The Four Quaker Questions

This is an old Quaker activity which Serendipity has adapted over the years. Go around the group and share your answers to the questions, everyone answering #1. Then, everyone answers #2, etc. This ice-breaker has been known to take between 30 and 60 minutes for some groups.

1. Where were you living between the ages of 7 and 12, and what were the winters like then?

2. How was your home heated during that time?

3. What was the center of warmth in your life when you were a child? (It could be a place in the house, a time of year, a person, etc.)

4. When did God become a "warm" person to you ... and how did it happen?

# KWIZ Show

Like a TV quiz show, someone from the group picks a category and reads the four questions—pausing to let the others in the group guess before revealing the answer. When the first person is finished, everyone adds up the money they won by guessing right. Go around the group and have each person take a category. The person with the most money at the end wins. To begin, ask one person to choose a CATEGORY and read out loud the $1 question. Before answering, let everyone try to GUESS the answer. When everyone has guessed, the person answers the question, and anyone who guessed right puts $1 in the margin, etc. until the first person has read all four questions in the CATEGORY.

# Clothes

**For $1:** I'm more likely to shop at:
❏ Sears ❏ Saks Fifth Avenue

**For $2:** I feel more comfortable wearing:
❏ formal clothes
❏ casual clothes
❏ sport clothes
❏ grubbies

**For $3:** In buying clothes, I look for:
❏ fashion / style
❏ price
❏ name brand
❏ quality

**For $4:** In buying clothes, I usually:
❏ shop all day for a bargain
❏ go to one store, but try on everything
❏ buy the first thing I try on
❏ buy without trying it on

# Tastes

**For $1:** In music, I am closer to:
❏ Bach ❏ Beatles

**For $2:** In furniture, I prefer:
❏ Early American
❏ French Provincial
❏ Scandinavian—contemporary
❏ Hodgepodge—little of everything

**For $3:** My favorite choice of reading material is:
❏ science fiction ❏ sports
❏ mystery ❏ romance

**For $4:** If I had $1,000 to splurge, I would buy:
❏ one original painting
❏ two numbered prints
❏ three reproductions and an easy chair
❏ four cheap imitations, an easy chair and a color TV

# Travel

**For $1:** For travel, I prefer:
❏ excitement ❏ enrichment

**For $2:** On a vacation, my lifestyle is:
❏ go-go all the time
❏ slow and easy
❏ party every night and sleep in

**For $3:** In packing for a trip, I include:
❏ toothbrush and change of underwear
❏ light bag and good book
❏ small suitcase and nice outfit
❏ all but the kitchen sink

**For $4:** If I had money to blow, I would choose:
❏ one glorious night in a luxury hotel
❏ a weekend in a nice hotel
❏ a full week in a cheap motel
❏ two weeks camping in the boon-docks

# Habits

**For $1:** I am more likely to squeeze the toothpaste:
❏ in the middle    ❏ from the end

**For $2:** If I am lost, I will probably:
❏ stop and ask directions
❏ check the map
❏ find the way by driving around

**For $3:** I read the newspaper starting with the:
❏ front page
❏ funnies
❏ sports
❏ entertainment section

**For $4:** When I get ready for bed, I put my clothes:
❏ on a hanger in the closet
❏ folded neatly over a chair
❏ into a hamper or clothes basket
❏ on the floor

# Shows

**For $1:** I am more likely to:
❏ go see a first-run movie
❏ rent a video at home

**For $2:** On TV, my first choice is:
❏ news
❏ sports
❏ sitcoms

**For $3:** If a show gets too scary, I will usually:
❏ go to the restroom
❏ close my eyes
❏ clutch a friend
❏ love it

**For $4:** In movies, I prefer:
❏ romantic comedies
❏ serious drama
❏ action films
❏ Disney animation

# Food

**For $1:** I prefer to eat at a:
❏ fast-food restaurant
❏ fancy restaurant

**For $2:** On the menu, I look for something:
❏ familiar
❏ different
❏ way-out

**For $3:** When eating chicken, my preference is a:
❏ drumstick
❏ wing
❏ breast
❏ gizzard

**For $4:** I draw the line when it comes to eating:
❏ frog legs
❏ snails
❏ raw oysters
❏ Rocky Mountain oysters

# Work

**For $1:** I prefer to work at a job that is:
❏ too big to handle
❏ too small to be challenging

**For $2:** The job I find most unpleasant to do is:
❏ cleaning the house
❏ working in the yard
❏ balancing the checkbook

**For $3:** In choosing a job, I look for:
❏ salary
❏ security
❏ fulfillment
❏ working conditions

**For $4:** If I had to choose between these jobs, I would choose:
❏ pickle inspector at processing plant
❏ complaint officer at department store
❏ bedpan changer at hospital
❏ personnel manager in charge of firing

# Let Me Tell You About My Day

What was your day like today? Use one of the characters below to help you describe your day to the group. Feel free to elaborate.

**GREEK TRAGEDY**
It was classic, not a dry eye in the house.

**EPISODE OF THREE STOOGES**
I was Larry, trapped between Curly and Moe.

**SOAP OPERA**
I didn't think these things could happen, until it happened to me.

**ACTION ADVENTURE**
When I rode onto the scene, everybody noticed.

**BIBLE EPIC**
Cecil B. DeMille couldn't have done it any better.

**LATE NIGHT NEWS**
It might as well have been broadcast over the airwaves.

**BORING LECTURE**
The biggest challenge of the day was staying awake.

**PROFESSIONAL WRESTLING MATCH**
I feel as if Hulk Hogan's been coming after me.

**FIREWORKS DISPLAY**
It was spectacular.

# Music in My Life

Put an *"X"* on the first line below—somewhere between the two extremes—to indicate how you are feeling right now. Share your answers, and then repeat this process down the list. If you feel comfortable, briefly explain your response.

IN MY PERSONAL LIFE, I'M FEELING LIKE ...
**Blues in the Night**_____ **Feeling Groovy**

IN MY FAMILY LIFE, I'M FEELING LIKE ...
**Stormy Weather** _____ **The Sound of Music**

IN MY EMOTIONAL LIFE, I'M FEELING LIKE ...
**The Feeling Is Gone** _____ **On Eagle's Wings**

IN MY WORK, SCHOOL OR CAREER, I'M FEELING LIKE ...
**Take This Job and Shove It** _____ **The Future's So Bright I Gotta Wear Shades**

IN MY SPIRITUAL LIFE, I'M FEELING LIKE ...
**Sounds of Silence** _____ **Hallelujah Chorus**

# My Childhood Table

Try to recall the table where you ate most of your meals as a child, and the people who sat around that table. Use the questions below to describe these significant relationships, and how they helped to shape the person you are today.

1. What was the shape of the table?
2. Where did you sit?
3. Who else was at the table?
4. If you had to describe each person with a color, what would be the color of (for instance):
   - ❏ Your father? (e.g., dark blue, because he was conservative like IBM)
   - ❏ Your mother? (e.g., light green, because she reminded me of springtime)
5. If you had to describe the atmosphere at the table with a color, what would you choose? (e.g., bright orange, because it was warm and light)
6. Who was the person at the table who praised you and made you feel special?
7. Who provided the spiritual leadership in your home?

# Home Improvement

Take inventory of your own life. Bob Munger, in his booklet *My Heart—Christ's Home*, describes the areas of a person's life as the rooms of a house. Give yourself a grade on each room as follows, then share with the others your best and worst grade.

    ❒ A = excellent        ❒ C = passing, needs a little dusting
    ❒ B = good             ❒ D = passing, but needs a lot of improvement

LIBRARY: This room is in your mind—what you allow to go into it and come out of it. It is the "control room" of the entire house.

DINING ROOM: Appetites, desires; those things your mind and spirit feed on for nourishment.

DRAWING ROOM: This is where you draw close to God—seeking time with him daily, not just in times of distress or need.

WORKSHOP: This room is where your gifts, talents and skills are put to work for God—by the power of the Spirit.

RUMPUS ROOM: The social area of your life; the things you do to amuse yourself and others.

HALL CLOSET: The one secret place that no one knows about, but is a real stumbling block in your walk in the Spirit.

# How Is It With Your Soul?

John Wesley, the founder of the Methodist Church, asked his "class meetings" to check in each week at their small group meeting with this question: "How is it with your soul?" To answer this question, choose one of these four allegories to explain the past week in your life:

WEATHER:    For example: "This week has been mostly cloudy, with some thunderstorms at midweek. Right now, the weather is a little brighter ..."

MUSIC:    For example: "This past week has been like heavy rock music—almost too loud. The sound seems to reverberate off the walls."

COLOR:    For example: "This past week has been mostly fall colors—deep orange, flaming red and pumpkin."

SEASON OF THE YEAR:    For example: "This past week has been like springtime. New signs of life are beginning to appear on the barren trees, and a few shoots of winter wheat are breaking through the frozen ground."

# My Spiritual Journey

The half-finished sentences below are designed to help you share your spiritual story. Ask one person to finish all the sentences. Then move to the next person, etc. If you are short on time, have only one person tell their story in this session.

1. RELIGIOUS BACKGROUND: My spiritual story begins in my home as a child, where the religious training was ...

2. CHURCH: The church that I went to as a child was ...

3. SIGNIFICANT PERSON: The person who had the greatest influence on my spiritual formation was ...

4. PERSONAL ENCOUNTER: The first time God became more than just a name to me was when ...

5. JOURNEY: Since my personal encounter with God, my Christian life might be described as ...

6. PRESENT: On a scale from 1 to 10, I would describe my spiritual energy level right now as a ...

7. NEXT STEP: The thing I need to work on right now in my spiritual life is ...

# Bragging Rights

Check your group for bragging rights in these categories.

❏ SPEEDING TICKETS: the person with the most speeding tickets
❏ BROKEN BONES: the person with the most broken bones
❏ STITCHES: the person with the most stitches
❏ SCARS: the person with the longest scar
❏ FISH OR GAME: the person who claims they caught the largest fish or killed the largest animal
❏ STUNTS: the person with the most death-defying story
❏ IRON: the person who can pump the most iron

# Personal Habits

Have everyone in your group finish the sentence on the first category by putting an "*X*" somewhere between the two extremes (e.g., on HOUSEWORK ... I would put myself closer to "Where's the floor?"). Repeat this process down the list as time permits.

ON HOUSEWORK, I AM SOMEWHERE BETWEEN:
Eat off the floor_____Where's the floor?

ON COOKING, I AM SOMEWHERE BETWEEN:
Every meal is an act of worship_____Make it fast and hold the frills

ON EXERCISING, I AM SOMEWHERE BETWEEN:
Workout every morning_____Click the remote

ON SHOPPING, I AM SOMEWHERE BETWEEN:
Shop all day for a bargain_____Only the best

ON EATING, I AM SOMEWHERE BETWEEN:
You are what you eat_____Eat, drink and be merry

# American Graffiti

If Hollywood made a movie about your life on the night of your high school prom, what would be needed? Let each person in your group have a few minutes to recall these details. If you have more than four or five in your group, ask everyone to choose two or three topics to talk about.

1. LOCATION: Where were you living?
2. WEIGHT: How much did you weigh—soaking wet?
3. PROM: Where was it held?
4. DATE: Who did you go with?
5. CAR / TRANSPORTATION: How did you get there?
   (If you used a car, what was the model, year, color, condition?)
6. ATTIRE: What did you wear?
7. PROGRAM: What was the entertainment?
8. AFTERWARD: What did you do afterward?
9. HIGHLIGHT: What was the highlight of the evening?
10. HOMECOMING: If you could go back and visit your high school, who would you like to see?

# Group Orchestra

Read out loud the first item and let everyone nominate the person in your group for this musical instrument in your group orchestra. Then, read aloud the next instrument, and call out another name, etc.

ANGELIC HARP: Soft, gentle, melodious, wooing with heavenly sounds.

OLD-FASHIONED WASHBOARD: Nonconforming, childlike and fun.

PLAYER PIANO: Mischievous, raucous, honky-tonk—delightfully carefree.

KETTLEDRUM: Strong, vibrant, commanding when needed but usually in the background.

PASSIONATE CASTANET: Full of Spanish fervor—intense and always upbeat.

STRADIVARIUS VIOLIN: Priceless, exquisite, soul-piercing—with the touch of the master.

FLUTTERING FLUTE: Tender, lighthearted, wide-ranging and clear as crystal.

SCOTTISH BAGPIPES: Forthright, distinctive and unmistakable.

SQUARE DANCE FIDDLE: Folksy, down-to-earth, toe-tapping—sprightly and full of energy.

ENCHANTING OBOE: Haunting, charming, disarming—even the cobra is harmless with this sound.

MELLOW CELLO: Deep, sonorous, compassionate—adding body and depth to the orchestra.

PIPE ORGAN: Grand, magnificent, rich—versatile and commanding.

HERALDING TRUMPET: Stirring, lively, invigorating—signaling attention and attack.

CLASSICAL GUITAR: Contemplative, profound, thoughtful *and* thought-provoking.

ONE-MAN BAND: Able to do many things well, all at once.

COMB AND TISSUE PAPER: Makeshift, original, uncomplicated—homespun and creative.

SWINGING TROMBONE: Warm, rich—great in solo or background support.

# Broadway Show

Imagine for a moment that your group has been chosen to produce a Broadway show, and you have to choose people from your group for all of the jobs for this production. Have someone read out loud the job description for the first job below—PRODUCER. Then, let everyone in your group call out the name of the person in your group who would best fit this job. (You don't have to agree.) Then read the job description for the next job and let everyone nominate another person, etc. You only have 10 minutes for this assignment, so move fast.

PRODUCER: Typical Hollywood business tycoon; extravagant, big-budget, big-production magnate in the Steven Spielberg style.

DIRECTOR: Creative, imaginative brains who coordinates the production and draws the best out of others.

HEROINE: Beautiful, captivating, everybody's heart throb; defenseless when men are around, but nobody's fool.

HERO: Tough, macho, champion of the underdog, knight in shining armor; defender of truth.

COMEDIAN: Childlike, happy-go-lucky, outrageously funny, keeps everyone laughing.

CHARACTER PERSON: Rugged individualist, outrageously different, colorful, adds spice to any surrounding.

FALL GUY: Easy-going, nonchalant character who wins the hearts of everyone by being the "foil" of the heavy characters.

TECHNICAL DIRECTOR: The genius for "sound and lights"; creates the perfect atmosphere.

COMPOSER OF LYRICS: Communicates in music what everybody understands; heavy into feelings, moods, outbursts of energy.

PUBLICITY AGENT: Advertising and public relations expert; knows all the angles, good at one-liners, a flair for "hot" news.

VILLAIN: The "bad guy" who really is the heavy for the plot, forces others to think, challenges traditional values; out to destroy anything artificial or hypocritical.

AUTHOR: Shy, aloof; very much in touch with feelings, sensitive to people, puts into words what others only feel.

STAGEHAND: Supportive, behind-the-scenes person who makes things run smoothly; patient and tolerant.

# Wild Predictions

Try to match the people in your group to the crazy forecasts below. (Don't take it too seriously; it's meant to be fun!) Read out loud the first item and ask everyone to call out the name of the person who is most likely to accomplish this feat. Then, read the next item and ask everyone to make a new prediction, etc.

THE PERSON IN OUR GROUP MOST LIKELY TO ...

Make a million selling Beanie Babies over the Internet

Become famous for designing new attire for sumo wrestlers

Replace Vanna White on *Wheel of Fortune*

Appear on *The Tonight Show* to exhibit an acrobatic talent

Move to a desert island

Discover a new use for underarm deodorant

Succeed David Letterman as host of *The Late Show*

Substitute for John Madden as Fox's football color analyst

Appear on the cover of *Muscle & Fitness Magazine*

Become the newest member of the Spice Girls

Work as a bodyguard for Rush Limbaugh at Feminist convention

Write a best-selling novel based on their love life

Be a dance instructor on a cruise ship for wealthy, well-endowed widows

Win the blue ribbon at the state fair for best Rocky Mountain oyster recipe

Land a job as head librarian for Amazon.com

Be the first woman to win the Indianapolis 500

Open the Clouseau Private Detective Agency

# Career Placements

Read the list of career choices aloud and quickly choose someone in your group for each job—based upon their unique gifts and talents. Have fun!

SPACE ENVIRONMENTAL ENGINEER: in charge of designing the bathrooms on space shuttles

SCHOOL BUS DRIVER: for junior high kids in New York City (earplugs supplied)

WRITER: of an "advice to the lovelorn" column in Hollywood

SUPERVISOR: of a complaint department for a large automobile dealership and service department

ANIMAL PSYCHIATRIST: for French poodles in a fashionable suburb of Paris

RESEARCH SCIENTIST: studying the fertilization patterns of the dodo bird—now extinct

SAFARI GUIDE: in the heart of Africa—for wealthy widows and eccentric bachelors

LITTLE LEAGUE BASEBALL COACH: in Mudville, Illinois—last year's record was 0 and 12

MANAGER: of your local McDonald's during the holiday rush with 210 teenage employees

LIBRARIAN: for the Walt Disney Hall of Fame memorabilia

CHOREOGRAPHER: for the Dallas Cowboys cheerleaders

NURSE'S AIDE: at a home for retired Sumo wrestlers

SECURITY GUARD: crowd control officer at a rock concert

ORGANIZER: of paperwork for Congress

PUBLIC RELATIONS MANAGER: for Dennis Rodman

BODYGUARD: for Rush Limbaugh on a speaking tour of feminist groups

TOY ASSEMBLY PERSON: for a toy store over the holidays

# You and Me, Partner

Think of the people in your group as you read over the list of activities below. If you had to choose someone from your group to be your partner, who would you choose to do these activities with? Jot down each person's name beside the activity. You can use each person's name only once and you have to use everyone's name once—so think it through before you jot down their names. Then, let one person listen to what others chose for them. Then, move to the next person, etc., around your group.

WHO WOULD YOU CHOOSE FOR THE FOLLOWING?

_____ ENDURANCE DANCE CONTEST partner

_____ BOBSLED RACE partner for the Olympics

_____ TRAPEZE ACT partner

_____ MY UNDERSTUDY for my debut in a Broadway musical

_____ BEST MAN or MAID OF HONOR at my wedding

_____ SECRET UNDERCOVER AGENT copartner

_____ BODYGUARD for me when I strike it rich

_____ MOUNTAIN CLIMBING partner in climbing Mt. Everest

_____ ASTRONAUT to fly the space shuttle while I walk in space

_____ SAND CASTLE TOURNAMENT building partner

_____ PIT CREW foreman for entry in Indianapolis 500

_____ AUTHOR for my biography

_____ SURGEON to operate on me for a life-threatening cancer

_____ NEW BUSINESS START-UP partner

_____ TAG-TEAM partner for a professional wrestling match

_____ HEAVY-DUTY PRAYER partner

# My Gourmet Group

Here's a chance to pass out some much deserved praise for the people who have made your group something special. Ask one person to sit in silence while the others explain the delicacy they would choose to describe the contribution this person has made to your group. Repeat the process for each member of the group.

CAVIAR: That special touch of class and aristocratic taste that has made the rest of us feel like royalty.

PRIME RIB: Stable, brawny, macho, the generous mainstay of any menu; juicy, mouth-watering "perfect cut" for good nourishment.

IMPORTED CHEESE: Distinctive, tangy, mellow with age; adds depth to any meal.

VINEGAR AND OIL: Tart, witty, dry; a rare combination of healing ointment and pungent spice to add "bite" to the salad.

ARTICHOKE HEARTS: Tender and disarmingly vulnerable; whets the appetite for heartfelt sharing.

FRENCH PASTRY: Tempting, irresistible "creme de la creme" dessert; the connoisseur's delight for topping off a meal.

PHEASANT UNDER GLASS: Wild, totally unique, a rare dish for people who appreciate original fare.

CARAFE OF WINE: Sparkling, effervescent, exuberant and joyful; outrageously free and liberating to the rest of us.

ESCARGOT AND OYSTERS: Priceless treasures of the sea once out of their shells; succulent, delicate and irreplaceable.

FRESH FRUIT: Vine-ripened, energy-filled, invigorating; the perfect treat after a heavy meal.

ITALIAN ICE CREAMS: Colorful, flavorful, delightfully childlike; the unexpected surprise in our group.

# Thank You

How would you describe your experience with this group? Choose one of the animals below that best describes how your experience in this group affected your life. Then share your responses with the group.

WILD EAGLE: You have helped to heal my wings, and taught me how to soar again.

TOWERING GIRAFFE: You have helped me to hold my head up and stick my neck out, and reach over the fences I have built.

PLAYFUL PORPOISE: You have helped me to find a new freedom and a whole new world to play in.

COLORFUL PEACOCK: You have told me that I'm beautiful; I've started to believe it, and it's changing my life.

SAFARI ELEPHANT: I have enjoyed this new adventure, and I'm not going to forget it, or this group; I can hardly wait for the next safari.

LOVABLE HIPPOPOTAMUS: You have let me surface and bask in the warm sunshine of God's love.

LANKY LEOPARD: You have helped me to look closely at myself and see some spots, and you still accept me the way I am.

DANCING BEAR: You have taught me to dance in the midst of pain, and you have helped me to reach out and hug again.

ALL-WEATHER DUCK: You have helped me to celebrate life—even in stormy weather—and to sing in the rain.

# Academy Awards

You have had a chance to observe the gifts and talents of the members of your group. Now you will have a chance to pass out some much deserved praise for the contribution that each member of the group has made to your life. Read out loud the first award. Then let everyone nominate the person they feel is the most deserving for that award. Then read the next award, etc., through the list. Have fun!

SPARK PLUG AWARD: for the person who ignited the group

DEAR ABBY AWARD: for the person who cared enough to listen

ROYAL GIRDLE AWARD: for the person who supported us

WINNIE THE POOH AWARD: for the warm, caring person when someone needed a hug

ROCK OF GIBRALTER AWARD: for the person who was strong in the tough times of our group

OPRAH AWARD: for the person who asked the fun questions that got us to talk

TED KOPPEL AWARD: for the person who asked the heavy questions that made us think

KING ARTHUR'S AWARD: for the knight in shining armor

PINK PANTHER AWARD: for the detective who made us deal with Scripture

NOBEL PEACE PRIZE: for the person who harmonized our differences of opinion without diminishing anyone

BIG MAC AWARD: for the person who showed the biggest hunger for spiritual things

SERENDIPITY CROWN: for the person who grew the most spiritually during the course—in your estimation

# You Remind Me of Jesus

Every Christian reflects the character of Jesus in some way. As your group has gotten to know each other, you can begin to see how each person demonstrates Christ in their very own personality. Go around the circle and have each person listen while others take turns telling that person what they notice in him or her that reminds them of Jesus. You may also want to tell them why you selected what you did.

YOU REMIND ME OF ...

JESUS THE HEALER: You seem to be able to touch someone's life with your compassion and help make them whole.

JESUS THE SERVANT: There's nothing that you wouldn't do for someone.

JESUS THE PREACHER: You share your faith in a way that challenges and inspires people.

JESUS THE LEADER: As Jesus had a plan for the disciples, you are able to lead others in a way that honors God.

JESUS THE REBEL: By doing the unexpected, you remind me of Jesus' way of revealing God in unique, surprising ways.

JESUS THE RECONCILER: Like Jesus, you have the ability to be a peacemaker between others.

JESUS THE TEACHER: You have a gift for bringing light and understanding to God's Word.

JESUS THE CRITIC: You have the courage to say what needs to be said, even if it isn't always popular.

JESUS THE SACRIFICE: Like Jesus, you seem willing to sacrifice anything to glorify God.

# Reflections

Take some time to evaluate the life of your group by using the statements below. Read the first sentence out loud and ask everyone to explain where they would put a dot between the two extremes. When you are finished, go back and give your group an overall grade in the category of Group Building, Bible Study and Mission.

## GROUP BUILDING

On celebrating life and having fun together, we were more like a ...
wet blanket _____ hot tub

On becoming a caring community, we were more like a ...
prickly porcupine_____cuddly teddy bear

## BIBLE STUDY

On sharing our spiritual stories, we were more like a ...
shallow pond _____spring-fed lake

On digging into Scripture, we were more like a ...
slow-moving snail _____voracious anteater

## MISSION

On inviting new people into our group, we were more like a ...
barbed-wire fence _____wide-open door

On stretching our vision for mission, we were more like an ...
ostrich _____eagle

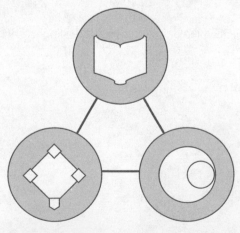

# Human Bingo / Party Mixer

After the leader says "Go!" circulate the room, asking people the things described in the boxes. If someone answers "Yes" to a question, have them sign their initials in that box. Continue until someone completes the entire card—or one row if you don't have that much time. You can only use someone's name twice, and you cannot use your own name on your card.

| can juggle | TP'd a house | never used an outhouse | sings in the shower | rec'd 6+ traffic tickets | paddled in school | watches Sesame Street |
|---|---|---|---|---|---|---|
| sleeps in church regularly | never changed a diaper | split pants in public | milked a cow | born out of the country | has been to Hawaii | can do the splits |
| watches soap operas | can touch tongue to nose | rode a motor-cycle | never ridden a horse | moved twice last year | sleeps on a waterbed | has hole in sock |
| walked in wrong restroom | loves classical music | skipped school | **FREE** | broke a leg | has a hot tub | loves eating sushi |
| is an only child | loves raw oysters | has a 3-inch + scar | doesn't wear PJ's | smoked a cigar | can dance the Charleston | weighs under 110 lbs. |
| likes writing poetry | still has tonsils | loves crossword puzzles | likes bubble baths | wearing Fruit of the Loom | doesn't use mouth-wash | often watches cartoons |
| kissed on first date | can wiggle ears | can play the guitar | plays chess regularly | reads the comics first | can touch palms to floor | sleeps with stuffed animal |

# Group Covenant

Any group can benefit from creating a group covenant. Reserve some time during one of the first meetings to discuss answers to the following questions. When everyone in the group has the same expectations for the group, everything runs more smoothly.

1.  The purpose of our group is:

2.  The goals of our group are:

3.  We will meet for _____ weeks, after which we will decide if we wish to continue as a group. If we do decide to continue, we will reconsider this covenant.

4.  We will meet _____ (weekly, every other week, monthly).

5.  Our meetings will be from _____ o'clock to _____ o'clock, and we will strive to start and end on time.

6.  We will meet at _____
    or rotate from house to house.

7.  We will take care of the following details:   ❏ child care   ❏ refreshments

8.  We agree to the following rules for our group:

    ❏  PRIORITY: While we are in this group, group meetings have priority.

    ❏  PARTICIPATION: Everyone is given the right to their own opinion and all questions are respected.

    ❏  CONFIDENTIALITY: Anything said in the meeting is not to be repeated outside the meeting.

    ❏  EMPTY CHAIR: The group stays open to new people and invites prospective members to visit the group.

    ❏  SUPPORT: Permission is given to call each other in times of need.

    ❏  ADVICE GIVING: Unsolicited advice is not allowed.

    ❏  MISSION: We will do all that is in our power to start a new group.

**3:10–14** Paul's next point (which he makes via a string of Old Testament quotes) is that law-keeping is ultimately futile, because no one is able to fulfill the *whole* Law—therefore no one is justified by the Law. Rather a curse hangs heavy upon them. Blessing comes by faith.

**3:10** According to Deuteronomy 27:26, anyone not keeping the *whole* Law is accursed.

***under a curse.*** That is, separated from God. This curse is the opposite of the blessing promised in verse 9.

***it is written.*** Paul continues to evoke the authority of Scripture.

**3:11** In verse 6 Paul argued that Abraham was justified by faith. "But was he not a special case?" it might be asked. Here Paul cites the same principle, given as a universal truth: right standing before God comes by faith.

**3:12** There is no connection between Law and faith. Law requires obedience, not belief.

**3:13** The only way to escape the curse laid upon a person because of personal (and inevitable) failure to keep the whole Law is by having another bear that curse for you. Since Christ had kept the whole Law (he was without sin), he had no curse on himself and so could bear the curse of others. He was "made sin for us" (as Paul says in 2 Cor. 5:21).

**3:14** Through Christ the promise given to Abraham came true at last: all who have faith in Christ (the descendant of Abraham) inherit the blessing of God's Spirit.

## The Law

1. This is a very loose term in that when it is used in Scripture it can refer to a variety of things. At times "the Law" is synonymous with "the Old Testament" (Rom. 3:19a). At other times it means the Pentateuch (Luke 24:44), i.e., the first five books of the Old Testament which contain the "Law of Moses." Then there is the so-called "oral law" which was the unwritten tradition that had developed to explain the meaning of the written law. It is against the oral law that Jesus took such exception.

2. The first-century Jew understood that God had revealed himself in the Law. In the Law one saw God's nature, will, and purpose. It was also understood that God could reveal himself through other means if he chose: angels, dreams, prophets and "voices." But the Jew also knew that in a particular and special way God had revealed himself through the written Law. The written Law was the primary means of revelation.

3. The Jews understood that the Law was to be obeyed. In fact, in the first century there were sects like the Pharisees that devoted themselves to one prime thing: the obedience of God's law. This was a full-time occupation, because for the Pharisees this meant not only observing the Old Testament precepts but all of the oral traditions. Thus, to be a Pharisee one had to be rich because you had no time left to work for a living.

4. The fact that they of all people had been the recipients of the Law gave the Jews a tremendous pride. But this was the problem. The Jews felt that by keeping the Law, they put God in their debt. God had to exempt them from negative judgment on the Final Day.

## THREE-PART AGENDA

| ICE-BREAKER | BIBLE STUDY | CARING TIME |
|---|---|---|
| 15 Minutes | 30 Minutes | 15–45 Minutes |

>  **LEADER:** *Check page M7 in the center section for a good ice-breaker, particularly if you have a new person at this meeting. In the Caring Time, is everyone sharing and are prayer requests being followed up?*

### TO BEGIN THE BIBLE STUDY TIME
(Choose 1 or 2)

1. What secret stuff did you keep locked up as a kid: A diary? Love notes? Sports cards? Other?

2. In your family, how far back can you trace your spiritual roots?

3. What federal or state law would you like to see enacted or removed?

### READ SCRIPTURE & DISCUSS
(If you don't have time for all the questions in this section, conclude the Bible Study [30 min.] by answering question #7.)

1. How important is it to have a will? What decisions are usually made in a will?

2. In what way is the human covenant of a will like God's covenant-promise with Abraham and his seed (v. 15)?

3. What is the promise that God gave to Abraham (see Gen. 12:2–3)? Who is the Seed through whom the promise to Abraham will be fulfilled (see note on v. 16)?

4. In what way is Abraham a spiritual father to us? In what family legacy can we share?

## The Law and the Promise

*¹⁵Brothers, let me take an example from everyday life. Just as no one can set aside or add to a human covenant that has been duly established, so it is in this case. ¹⁶The promises were spoken to Abraham and to his seed. The Scripture does not say "and to seeds," meaning many people, but "and to your seed,"ᵃ meaning one person, who is Christ. ¹⁷What I mean is this: The law, introduced 430 years later, does not set aside the covenant previously established by God and thus do away with the promise. ¹⁸For if the inheritance depends on the law, then it no longer depends on a promise; but God in his grace gave it to Abraham through a promise.*

*¹⁹What, then, was the purpose of the law? It was added because of transgressions until the Seed to whom the promise referred had come. The law was put into effect through angels by a mediator. ²⁰A mediator, however, does not represent just one party; but God is one.*

*²¹Is the law, therefore, opposed to the promises of God? Absolutely not! For if a law had been given that could impart life, then righteousness would certainly have come by the law. ²²But the Scripture declares that the whole world is a prisoner of sin, so that what was promised, being given through faith in Jesus Christ, might be given to those who believe.*

*²³Before this faith came, we were held prisoners by the law, locked up until faith should be revealed. ²⁴So the law was put in charge to lead us to Christᵇ that we might be justified by faith. ²⁵Now that faith has come, we are no longer under the supervision of the law.*

ᵃ16 Gen. 12:7; 13:15; 24:7      ᵇ24 Or *charge until Christ came*

5. Since the Law did not replace the promise, what was its purpose?

6. What kinds of legalism do Christians fall prey to? How is your faith liberating you from this spiritual bondage?

7. On a scale of 1 to 10, what number would show up on your "faith meter" for this past week? Where do you need to have more faith in your life?

## CARING TIME

(Choose 1 or 2 of these questions before closing in prayer. Be sure to pray for the empty chair.)

1. It's not too late to have someone new come to this group. Who can you invite for next week?

2. Congratulations! You're over halfway through this study. What do you look forward to about coming to this group?

3. How can this group pray for you in the coming week?

**3:15–18** Having argued from experience and from Scripture for the primacy of faith, Paul now argues the same point from human reason. He asks the Galatians to think about how wills are made. His point is that once established, no one can alter a will. Likewise, the covenant given by God to Abraham cannot be altered. So the Law which was given to Moses several centuries later has no impact on this covenant-promise. The promised blessings came to Abraham's true children, not because they earned them via law-keeping (there is no legal right here), but because they came by grace without conditions.

---

*Spiritual life flows out of right relationship to God and this does not come about as a result of observing the Law, no matter how true that law might be. If the Law could give life, Christ didn't need to die.*

---

**3:15 *an example.*** In his appeal to reason, Paul points to judicial practices by way of analogy. A will cannot be annulled by law.

***no one can set aside.*** "When a deed of settlement is properly signed, sealed, and delivered and the property legally conveyed, not even the original owner can revoke or alter its terms" (Bruce).

***or add to.*** Under Roman law a "testator could add a codicil at any time that he chose, but after his death (or before it, for that matter) nobody else might do so" (Bruce).

***covenant.*** Akin to a last will and testament in which one's descendants are promised certain things. In this case the blessings promised to the children of Abraham are, according to Paul, justification by faith and the gift of the Spirit (3:10–14).

**3:16** A point of grammar introduces a key distinction. God's promises to Abraham were not for *all* his many descendants, but more specifically, for his one crucial descendant: the Messiah. The blessings are then channeled outward to all who believe—Jew or Gentile—through Jesus the Messiah.

**3:17** The prior covenant is unaffected by the later Law.

***430 years later.*** The Law was given much later, during the time of Moses.

**3:18 *inheritance.*** Promises made to a person's descendants.

***grace.*** God's promises to Abraham had nothing to do with law or obligations. It was a pure gift without conditions.

**3:19 *What, then, was the purpose of the law?*** If the promises came by faith, what about the Law? What purpose did it have? This is a burning question to the Judaizers (for whom the Law was their whole life), because they felt that it reflected perfectly God's will.

***It was added ... until.*** Paul answers that the Law was *temporary*. Its purpose was to make people aware of their sin, but when the Messiah came its function would cease. "That the promulgation of specific enactments creates a corresponding category of specific violations, with opportunity (and perhaps temptation) to commit these violations, is a fact of human experience. But Paul's statement goes beyond this: the *purpose* of the law was to increase the sum-total of transgression" (Bruce).

***by a mediator.*** On the basis of Deuteronomy 33:2, it was concluded that the Law was given to Moses at Mt. Sinai by the angels who accompanied God. Paul's point is that a word that came indirectly from God is of less significance than one that came directly, as did God's promises to Abraham.

**3:21** The Law and the promises (Moses and Abraham) are not in opposition. But Paul knew as a former Pharisee that the Law could not and did not impart life. The promised life only came by faith. "Paul's method of reasoning appears to be as follows. Law is associated with curses, the very antithesis of life. Law, in fact, could only show that man did not qualify for life. It has no power to bring to life that which it had pronounced dead. That is because it is contrary to the nature of law to give life. ... (Paul's) purpose is to show that the reasons for the superiority of promise over law is not due to any failure on the part of the latter to achieve what it was designed to do. It had brought no life because it had never been intended for that purpose" (Guthrie).

> *The Law cannot impart life but it does reveal the bondage of human beings to sin and thus drives them to faith as their only hope.*

*life.* Spiritual life flows out of right relationship to God and this does not come about as a result of observing the Law, no matter how true that law might be. If the Law could give life, Christ didn't need to die (2:21).

**3:22 *prisoner of sin.*** "The written law is the officiant who locks the law-breaker up in the prison house of which sin is the jailor" (Bruce).

**3:23–25** Paul concludes his argument by showing how Christ liberates people from the Law.

**3:23 *prisoners by the law.*** Now the Law is the jailor, and not sin (as in v. 22). "To be 'under law' is in practice to be 'under sin'—not because law, while forbidding sin, stimulates the very thing that it forbids" (Bruce).

**3:24–25** The Law cannot impart life, but it does reveal the bondage of people to sin and thus drives them to faith as their only hope.

**3:24 *put in charge.*** The Law is now pictured as a tutor. The same word is used for household slaves whose responsibility it was to look after the young men in the family until they reached the age of accountability. Such "tutors" were more involved in discipline than education, however. The Law functioned in the same way. It "looked after us" until Christ came, whereupon its task was finished.

**3:25 *faith has come.*** Paul will explain in verses 26–27 what this "coming of age" means for the person of faith.

## The Problem With Religious People

Not many people liked the Jews in the first century. The Jews appeared to them to be aloof, arrogant and self-righteous. It felt like they were always looking down their noses at you and constantly shaking their heads in reproof. That's the problem with religious people: Because we do really try to do what is right, we have a tendency to look down on those who don't do what (we consider) is right.

Looked at from the point of view of the Jew, such an attitude was not inappropriate. The Jews really tried to follow the Law and it wasn't easy. And when they looked around, they saw all those other people messing around, doing nasty things, enjoying themselves illicitly. "Well, who would not be scornful? Keeping the law was hard, demanding work. You couldn't do all the things you wanted to do. So, sure, you've earned the right to look down on those decadent folks."

Of course the problem with this is that the other folks are going to resent our censoriousness. They are probably more aware of their own "wrong-doing" than we realize, but they are not about to let us know that.

What the Jews had to do (and what we need to do) is to stop trying so hard—but rather rest in God's forgiving grace, and love other people (because God loves us).

# 8 Sons of God—Galatians 3:26–4:7

## THREE-PART AGENDA

**ICE-BREAKER**
15 Minutes

**BIBLE STUDY**
30 Minutes

**CARING TIME**
15–45 Minutes

>  **LEADER:** *Have you started working with your group about your mission—for instance, by having them review pages M3 and M6 in the center section? If you have a new person at the meeting, remember to do an appropriate ice-breaker from the center section.*

## TO BEGIN THE BIBLE STUDY TIME
(Choose 1 or 2)

1. What is your clothes-shopping style: Laid-back and fun? Efficient and goal-oriented? Avoid at all costs? Other?

2. What heirloom would you like to pass on to future generations of your family?

3. How affectionate was, or is, your relationship with your parents?

## READ SCRIPTURE & DISCUSS
(If you don't have time for all the questions in this section, conclude the Bible Study [30 min.] by answering question #7.)

1. As a child of God, what would you like to thank your heavenly Father for?

2. How would you explain to a non-Christian what it takes to become a child of God?

3. What effect does being "in Christ" have on relationships among believers (3:28)?

## Sons of God

*²⁶You are all sons of God through faith in Christ Jesus, ²⁷for all of you who were baptized into Christ have clothed yourselves with Christ. ²⁸There is neither Jew nor Greek, slave nor free, male nor female, for you are all one in Christ Jesus. ²⁹If you belong to Christ, then you are Abraham's seed, and heirs according to the promise.*

**4** *What I am saying is that as long as the heir is a child, he is no different from a slave, although he owns the whole estate. ²He is subject to guardians and trustees until the time set by his father. ³So also, when we were children, we were in slavery under the basic principles of the world. ⁴But when the time had fully come, God sent his Son, born of a woman, born under law, ⁵to redeem those under law, that we might receive the full rights of sons. ⁶Because you are sons, God sent the Spirit of his Son into our hearts, the Spirit who calls out, "Abba,ᵃ Father." ⁷So you are no longer a slave, but a son; and since you are a son, God has made you also an heir.*

ᵃ6 Aramaic for *Father*

4. What are some social and cultural barriers to the unity of Christians in our time? How can you help to bring down these barriers in your own life?

5. How is being under the Law like being an heir who is still a minor (4: 1–3)?

6. How has God intervened to alter human history and adopt us as full heirs (4:4–5)? (See note on 4:4 to help appreciate God's marvelous plan and timing.)

7. How affectionate is your relationship with God right now: Very close, like a child and their Daddy (or "Abba"—4:6)? Sort of close, like a parent and grown child who just "keep in touch"? Strained, like a parent and child who have had a "falling out"?

## CARING TIME
(Choose 1 or 2 of these questions before closing in prayer. Be sure to pray for the empty chair.)

1. What is something you are looking forward to this week?

2. What is your dream for the future mission of this group?

3. In what specific way can this group pray for you this week?

**Summary.** Paul emphasizes the new family relationship with God that all types of people can enjoy through faith in Christ. Law has nothing to do with it.

**3:26 *You.*** Jewish and Gentile believers; the same group addressed as *we* in 3:23–25.

**3:26 *sons of God.*** With the advent of faith (3:25) came a whole new possibility: to become a child of God in a real, immediate way. Paul is not speaking here of a generalized "everybody is a child of God because God is the father of the human race" sort of reality. Rather it is quite a specific son/daughtership which results from having become linked to his unique Son, Jesus Christ.

***in Christ Jesus.*** A distinctive Pauline phrase by which he seeks to express the faith-union between Jesus and the believer. This includes, but transcends, mere affirmation on a cognitive level that Jesus is Lord of the Universe. There is also an inner, mystical experience both for individual believers and for the Christian community as a whole.

**3:27 *baptized.*** A common water rite in Judaism; one of three acts by which a person became a Jew; picked up and given new meaning (repentance and remission of sins) by John the Baptist; and later used by the Christian church as the visible, outward sign of admission into the Christian community. Baptism is not that which replaced circumcision as the new means to salvation. Paul would have pointed to his conversion experience on the Damascus road as the point at which he was justified by faith. His baptism followed later. In fact, "repentance and faith, with baptism in water and reception of the Spirit, followed by first communion, constituted one complex experience of Christian initiation (so that) what is true of the experience as a whole can in practice be predicated of any element in it. The creative agent, however, is the Spirit. Baptism in water *per se* is no guarantee of salvation as the presence of the Spirit is" (Bruce).

***clothed.*** This image may spring from the practice by the early church of removing old garments prior to baptism and then donning a new white robe after baptism. The idea here is of being identified with Christ, as in Job 29:14 where Job said, "I put on righteousness as my clothing" to indicate that he was identified with righteousness.

**3:28 *Jew nor Greek.*** From the first-century Jewish perspective, the cleavage between Jew and Greek was of the deepest sort. Jewish contempt for non-Jews was immense. Gentiles, they said, had been created by God as fuel for the fires of hell. For that barrier to have fallen was simply incredible.

***slave nor free.*** Although the some 60 million slaves virtually ran the Roman Empire, they were generally regarded as mere things, without rights, subject to any whim of their masters. This was another barrier broken down by Christ.

***male nor female.*** A woman had few if any rights in either first-century Judaism or Greco-Roman culture. She belonged to her husband and he could treat her as he chose, including divorcing her with ease. This barrier, too, Christ removed so that in the same way a Gentile or a slave could exercise leadership in the church, so too could women.

***one in Christ Jesus.*** In morning prayer, a Jewish man thanked God that he had not been made a Gentile, a slave, or a woman. (The idea was not to disparage such people, but to express gratitude to God that as a man, he was not disqualified as they were from certain religious privileges.) Paul reverses this prayer. The traditional distinctions are finished. In Christ all are one. This was a radical principle in his time (and ours) when deep division was common. It serves as a universal statement of what is meant to be.

**3:29 *Abraham's seed.*** Perhaps Paul's opponents argued that it was vital for Gentile Christians to become sons of Abraham by circumcision. He counters by pointing out that they are already sons of Abraham by virtue of their union with Christ.

> *Not only did the Son experience the humiliation of Incarnation (he was born), but also the frustration of bondage to the very Law from which he came to free humanity.*

**4:1–2** Paul has already pointed out that to live under the law is like being in prison (3:23) or like being under the watchful eye of a strict tutor (3:24). Now he adds a third, related image: it is also like being a slave. In theory the child is heir to the whole estate but in fact he is no better off than a slave (because he is under the strict control of his guardian and has no access to the inheritance).

**4:1** *What I am saying.* In order to illustrate further the difference between the former time of spiritual immaturity and the new experience of freedom, Paul uses another analogy. The Law is like a caretaker appointed to look after the affairs of a minor child until they come of age.

*a child.* A minor; one who has in a legal sense not yet come of age.

*a slave.* In the sense of being under the absolute control of the father and not free to act on one's own.

**4:2** *guardians and trustees.* In his will, a Roman father appointed a guardian who looked after the child until he came of age at 14. Then a curator looked after the child's affairs until age 25.

*until the time set.* The father had some discretion as to when the child received the inheritance.

**4:3** *basic principles.* This Greek word refers to the rudimentary elements out of which more complex structures are built; as, for example, the letters of the alphabet which are used to form words and sentences. Paul seems to be referring here to the Law (as in 3:23). Before Christ came Jews were under bondage to the "rudimentary notions of the world" (Metzger). It was as if they remained a bunch of infants preoccupied with the ABCs of life, unaware of the real meaning of things.

**4:4** *when the time had fully come.* Finally, the long history of God's revelation reaches a culminating point: Jesus is sent. In fact, it was the perfect point in history for such an event. For the first time the whole world was at peace, united under one power—Rome. There was a common tongue—Greek; and a network of first-rate roads spanning the empire so that the message could spread. There was also widespread anxiety and questing for truth—the temple cults and philosophical systems having shown themselves to be barren of meaning. Therefore, the message would be heard eagerly. And clusters of Jews were scattered across the

empire. Though not necessarily liked nor understood, they were widely respected for their strict morality and lofty theology. The Gospel spread fastest via their synagogues and then out into the pagan environment around them.

> *To become a child of God means that a person receives the Spirit of God; to one's new, external status is added new, internal experience of God's love and power.*

*born of a woman.* The God of the Universe, incredibly, sends his own divine, unique Son down through time and space into history as a human baby. The divine invades the natural.

*born under law.* Not only did the Son experience the humiliation of Incarnation (he was born), but also the frustration of bondage to the very Law from which he came to free humanity.

**4:5** *to redeem those under law.* His purpose was to release the prisoners, to free the slaves, to bear the curse of the Law himself. Jesus delivered people from the Law to son/daughtership.

*full rights of sons.* Literally, adoption, a widespread practice in the Greco-Roman world whereby a child became a member of a new family with equivalent rights to those born in the family.

**4:6** *sent the Spirit.* To become a child of God means that a person receives the Spirit of God; to one's new, external status is added new, internal experience of God's love and power.

*Abba.* The Aramaic word for father—literally, "Daddy." The adoptive children are not bound in a mere legal sense to this new Father; but a deep, affectionate relationship exists.

**4:7** *slave / son.* The Christian is no longer enslaved by the powers (4:3) but is freed to become a son or daughter of God. Their status changes from slave to child.

*heir.* As a child of God, one is the inheritor of all his promised blessings.

# 9 Paul's Concern—Galatians 4:8–20

## THREE-PART AGENDA

**ICE-BREAKER**
15 Minutes

**BIBLE STUDY**
30 Minutes

**CARING TIME**
15–45 Minutes

> *LEADER: To help you identify an Apprentice / Leader for a new small group (or if you have a new person at this meeting), see the listing of ice-breakers on page M7 of the center section.*

## TO BEGIN THE BIBLE STUDY TIME
(Choose 1 or 2)

1. Other than Christmas, what was your favorite holiday growing up?

2. Who would you like to go visit if you could leave tomorrow?

3. What is the most difficult illness you or a loved one has had?

## READ SCRIPTURE & DISCUSS
(If you don't have time for all the questions in this section, conclude the Bible Study [30 min.] by answering question #7.)

1. How do you relate to someone close to you whom you're worried about? How does your tone of voice change when you talk to them?

2. How does Paul express the following emotions as he writes these words: Personal frustration mixed with concern (v. 11)? Pleading (v. 12)? Nostalgia (vv. 13–15)? Self-pity (v. 16)? Jealousy (v. 17)? Compassion (v. 19)? Anxiety (v. 20)?

3. What are the "weak and miserable principles" (v. 9) that the Galatians are turning back to?

## Paul's Concern for the Galatians

*⁸Formerly, when you did not know God, you were slaves to those who by nature are not gods. ⁹But now that you know God—or rather are known by God—how is it that you are turning back to those weak and miserable principles? Do you wish to be enslaved by them all over again? ¹⁰You are observing special days and months and seasons and years! ¹¹I fear for you, that somehow I have wasted my efforts on you.*

*¹²I plead with you, brothers, become like me, for I became like you. You have done me no wrong. ¹³As you know, it was because of an illness that I first preached the gospel to you. ¹⁴Even though my illness was a trial to you, you did not treat me with contempt or scorn. Instead, you welcomed me as if I were an angel of God, as if I were Christ Jesus himself. ¹⁵What has happened to all your joy? I can testify that, if you could have done so, you would have torn out your eyes and given them to me. ¹⁶Have I now become your enemy by telling you the truth?*

*¹⁷Those people are zealous to win you over, but for no good. What they want is to alienate you from us, so that you may be zealous for them. ¹⁸It is fine to be zealous, provided the purpose is good, and to be so always and not just when I am with you. ¹⁹My dear children, for whom I am again in the pains of childbirth until Christ is formed in you, ²⁰how I wish I could be with you now and change my tone, because I am perplexed about you!*

4. What kind of illness did Paul have (see note on v. 14)? How did the Galatians respond? How can this group help those who are ill?

5. How does a relationship with God based on "performance" and keeping the rules take the joy out of the Christian life?

6. On a scale of 1 (don't ask) to 10 (my cup runneth over), how much joy is in your life?

7. Like the Galatians, have you slipped back into any bad habits or old ways, from which Christ once delivered you? Which ones? What can you do about it?

## CARING TIME
(Choose 1 or 2 of these questions before closing in prayer. Be sure to pray for the empty chair.)

1. Have you started to work on your group mission—to choose an Apprentice / Leader from this group to start a new group in the future? (See Mission / Multiplication on p. M3.)

2. If this group is helping to hold you accountable for something, how are you doing in that area? If not, what is something for which you would like this group to hold you accountable?

3. What prayer needs or praises would you like to share?

**4:8 you.** Now Paul addresses specifically the Gentile Christians in Galatia.

**are not gods.** In their pagan days they worshiped many entities (idols, animals, powers) that really were not gods.

**4:9 are known.** To know God is to be known by God—the relationship is reciprocal. By this phrase he also emphasizes that it was nothing the Gentiles did that brought about such a relationship. God took the initiative.

**turning back.** Paul can't imagine how they can turn from the experience of the living God to the bondage of pretend gods.

**weak and miserable.** Although these powers were once strong enough to enslave a person, now because of Christ's liberating work they are rendered impotent—unless people deliberately put themselves back under their control.

**principles.** The Gentiles, too, were under bondage to principles. This term was used to refer to the four physical elements—earth, air, fire and water. Since in the Greek worldview all such forces were understood to be animate, these principles came to be regarded as personal beings—angelic and demonic powers that were thought to rule the universe and influence the fate of individuals. Much pagan religion sought to tame and control these powerful entities.

**4:10** The Jews were rigorous in observing days (like the Sabbath), months (e.g., the "new moons" in Isa. 1:14 and the offerings in Num. 28:11-15), seasons (e.g., Passover), and years (e.g., the Sabbath Year in Lev. 25). "Since all these observations depend on astronomical calculations, they sprung in the last resort from the same kind of superstition as heathenism" (Neil). To observe such a sacred calendar is to put oneself once more under the power of the forces that control the calendar.

**observing.** Paul observed certain sacred events (Acts 20:16; 1 Cor. 16:8). But it is one thing for a Jew to continue in his ethnic tradition in a nonbinding way, and another for a group of Gentiles to adopt in a legalistic fashion the Jewish calendar.

**4:12–20** Paul breaks off the flow of his argument and makes a personal appeal to the Galatians.

**4:12 become like me.** When Paul was among them he was not bound by Jewish customs and practices. They, too, must avoid the trap of legalism.

**I became like you.** Perhaps Paul is referring to his willingness to become all things to all people in order to win them (1 Cor. 9:19–23). Certainly he did not live in a rigid, law-oriented way but was free to mingle in Gentile society.

**done me no wrong.** Paul harbors no resentment. What he has written is out of concern for their Christian faith.

**4:13–14** He reminds them of how they first received him.

**4:14 illness.** Some take this to be malaria, believing that Paul had contracted it in the lowlands around Pamphylia and then made his way into the highlands of Pisidian Antioch (in Galatia) in order to recover (Acts 13:13–14). Others have identified his illness as epilepsy; still others as ophthalmia (because in v. 15 the Galatians would have given their eyes to him). However, there is no way to be certain about his ailment.

**a trial to you.** For some reason the illness had made Paul repulsive in appearance.

**scorn.** Literally, "to spit out."

**an angel.** Perhaps there is an allusion to the time when Paul and Barnabas went to Lystra and were mistaken for gods (Acts 14:11–13). In any case, the contrast is between the greeting given an angel or Christ Jesus and their present attitude toward Paul.

**4:15 torn out your eyes.** Probably just an expression of deep gratitude; i.e., at that time there was nothing the Galatians would not have done for Paul.

**4:16** In contrast to their original affection they are now treating Paul as an enemy.

**4:17** The Judaizers are out to win adherents, even though by so doing they lure the Galatians from the true Gospel.

**4:18** "It is always good, he goes on, to be courted with honorable intentions, as you were 'courted' by me when I was present with you; but as it is, no sooner has my back been turned than you let someone else come and 'court' you with dishonorable intentions!" (Bruce).

**4:19** Paul often refers to himself as the father of spiritual children (1 Cor. 4:15). Here he plays the part of a mother, and so expresses his deep love and concern.

*My dear children.* Paul cannot mask his deep affection for them despite his deep distress over their actions.

*again.* For the second time he must endure the pangs of childbirth—first when he sought to bring them out of paganism and into new birth in Christ, and now as he seeks to bring their faith out of legalism.

*Christ is formed in you.* The metaphor is mixed but the point is clear. Paul's desire is that they come to possess Christlike characteristics.

**4:20** He wishes he could be with them in circumstances where he would not have to be so concerned about their welfare.

*change my tone.* Not that he retracts his strong words, rather he wants them to feel that they come in love.

## Laws by the Score

It all began simply enough. There were ten commandments. They defined God's intention for his people. They explained in broad, sweeping strokes how people should live. Simple enough ... except that there were only ten of them and with only *ten* commandments all sorts of questions about behavior are left unanswered.

So it was quite natural that over time rabbis would offer explanations and add amplifying statements so as to clarify the basic commandments. In time these teachings were collected together as a sort of running commentary on the original Ten Commandments. At first this was an oral tradition, kept alive by the extraordinary memories of the people. Eventually all this got written down—and then this written document was subject to scrutiny and yet more clarifying statements were written.

By the time of Jesus the whole business of law-keeping had gotten quite out of hand. Take the question of the Sabbath. "Remember the Sabbath day by keeping it holy" is how it was originally put. "Six days you shall labor and do all your work, but the seventh day is a Sabbath to the LORD your God. On it you shall not do any work ..." (Ex. 20:8–10). Fair enough. Don't work on the Sabbath ... but what is work? Here is where the trouble begins. By the time of Jesus there were thousands of petty rules and regulations. Work itself had been categorized under some 39 different headings.

It was even forbidden to heal on the Sabbath. Healing was work. You could give medical assistance but only if a life was in danger. A woman could be assisted in giving birth to a child, but if a wall fell on someone, only enough of it could be cleared away to ascertain if the person was dead or alive. If dead, then the body had to be left until the next day. Small ailments were left unattended. You couldn't splint a fracture or put cold water on a sprained ankle. You could bandage a cut but you couldn't put a salve on it, because the salve would provoke healing and healing was work! Now this is bondage to law! No wonder Jesus declared so forcefully: "The Sabbath was made for man, not man for the Sabbath!"—Adapted in part from materials in *The Gospel of Mark* by William Barclay.

# 10 Hagar & Sarah—Galatians 4:21–31

## THREE-PART AGENDA

**ICE-BREAKER**
15 Minutes

**BIBLE STUDY**
30 Minutes

**CARING TIME**
15–45 Minutes

> *LEADER: Check page M7 in the center section for a good ice-breaker, particularly if you have a new person at this meeting. Is your group working well together—with everyone "fielding their position" as shown on the team roster on page M5?*

## TO BEGIN THE BIBLE STUDY TIME
(Choose 1 or 2)

1. Where were you born? What details do you know about your birth?

2. What do you like to do when relatives visit?

3. What special quality do (or did) you appreciate about your mother or someone who is like a mother to you?

## READ SCRIPTURE & DISCUSS
(If you don't have time for all the questions in this section, conclude the Bible Study [30 min.] by answering question #7.)

1. What is one of your favorite Old Testament stories?

2. Why is the story in Genesis about Hagar and Sarah important to Paul's argument (see second note on v. 22)?

3. How does Hagar represent the covenant of Law given to the Jews through Moses on Mt. Sinai (v. 24)?

4. Why does Paul turn the tables on this story and indicate that the Jews are actually the ones in slavery with Hagar—their slave woman mother (v. 25)?

### Hagar and Sarah

*²¹Tell me, you who want to be under the law, are you not aware of what the law says? ²²For it is written that Abraham had two sons, one by the slave woman and the other by the free woman. ²³His son by the slave woman was born in the ordinary way; but his son by the free woman was born as the result of a promise.*

*²⁴These things may be taken figuratively, for the women represent two covenants. One covenant is from Mount Sinai and bears children who are to be slaves: This is Hagar. ²⁵Now Hagar stands for Mount Sinai in Arabia and corresponds to the present city of Jerusalem, because she is in slavery with her children. ²⁶But the Jerusalem that is above is free, and she is our mother. ²⁷For it is written:*

*"Be glad, O barren woman,*
  *who bears no children;*
*break forth and cry aloud,*
  *you who have no labor pains;*
*because more are the children of the*
      *desolate woman*
    *than of her who has a husband."*ᵃ

*²⁸Now you, brothers, like Isaac, are children of promise. ²⁹At that time the son born in the ordinary way persecuted the son born by the power of the Spirit. It is the same now. ³⁰But what does the Scripture say? "Get rid of the slave woman and her son, for the slave woman's son will never share in the inheritance with the free woman's son."*ᵇ *³¹Therefore, brothers, we are not children of the slave woman, but of the free woman.*

ᵃ*27 Isaiah 54:1*      ᵇ*30 Gen. 21:10*

5. What does verse 27 say figuratively about Sarah's children? How did the spiritual and numerical growth of the Gentiles fulfill this Scripture from Isaiah?

6. How does verse 30 give a stern warning to the Judaizers? What is God saying to *you* in this passage?

7. This past week, did you feel more like Hagar (a slave to rules) or Sarah (a free, loved and forgiven Christian)? How can you live out your freedom in Christ, and still please him with your sacrificial obedience?

## CARING TIME
(Choose 1 or 2 of these questions before closing in prayer.)

1. How are you doing at spending personal time in prayer and Bible study?

2. How is the group doing "fielding their positions," as shown on the team roster (p. M5)?

3. What would you like to share with the group for prayer this week?

**Summary.** Paul returns to his doctrinal argument. He does so by picking up the idea of childbirth (4:19) and developing a complex allegory based on the experience of Hagar and Sarah and their two sons, Ishmael and Isaac. His main thesis is that Judaism is based on the Law, while Christianity is based on the promises of God. The Law brings slavery, while the promises [of God] bring freedom.

**4:21 *are you not aware.*** If they insist on being under the Law, Paul wants them to be quite clear about the implications of this. Abraham had two sons. One was under bondage while the other was free. Paul will urge them to be like the child of the free woman and not be bound to the slavery of the Law.

**4:22 *it is written.*** Paul will make his case from Old Testament Scriptures.

***two sons.*** Sarah had failed to produce a son for Abraham and so decided to do so by proxy through her Egyptian servant, Hagar. This was, apparently, a recognized custom (Gen. 30:3–13). Ishmael was born in due course to the great delight of Abraham (Gen. 16:1–16; 17:18). However, some years later, God promised to give Abraham a son by Sarah and, indeed, a year later Isaac was born. When this happened, Sarah demanded that Abraham cast out Hagar and Ishmael. He did this with great distress, only after God promised that Ishmael would become the father of a great nation (the Arab tribes). The Ishmaelites eventually came to represent (for the Jews) all Gentiles—i.e., those excluded from God's covenants.

**4:23 *in the ordinary way.*** There was nothing exceptional about this birth.

***as the result of a promise.*** On the other hand, Isaac's birth was quite extraordinary; not at all to be expected in the course of nature. Both Abraham and Sarah were well beyond the usual age of childbearing.

**4:24 *figuratively.*** Literally, "as an allegory." An incident from the Old Testament is interpreted to have spiritual significance for the present because God is understood to operate in similar ways throughout history. Thus his action in Old Testament times prefigures his action in New Testament times.

***two covenants.*** The contrast is between Hagar (who represents the covenant of Law which was given to Moses on Mt. Sinai) and Sarah (who represents the covenant of promise given to Abraham). In contrast to the way the Judaizers understood the stories, the Jews were seen by Paul as descending from Hagar (since they were enslaved by the Law), while the Gentiles (and a minority of believing Jews) were understood to be Sarah's descendants (since they had been liberated from the Law by Christ and were therefore free). The Judaizers would have understood (and taught) these texts in reverse fashion. Hagar was the mother of the Gentiles who are enslaved to sin and outside the realm of God's covenants, while Sarah was the mother of the Jewish race who enjoyed all the benefits of God's covenant. In fact, the Judaizers probably appealed to the Galatians to be circumcised and so became a part of the covenant people which is why Paul deals with these texts in reverse fashion.

***covenant.*** A solemn agreement between God and people, in which he promises to be their God and they promise to be his people. The new covenant came through Christ. The old covenant was based on Law; the new on promises. In the old covenant, a heavy responsibility was placed on people to obey ("thou shalt not"), while in the new covenant the responsibility is God's ("I will") (Stott).

**4:25 *Mount Sinai.*** The mountain in Arabia upon which Moses received the Law.

> *A covenant is a solemn agreement between God and people, in which he promises to be their God and they promise to be his people. The new covenant came through Christ. The old covenant was based on Law; the new on promises.*

**to the present city of Jerusalem.** For Paul, Jerusalem represents contemporary Judaism with all its legalism.

**in slavery.** Just as Jerusalem was in slavery to Rome, the Jews were enslaved to the Law which had become an enormous burden (expressed in a multitude of regulations covering every conceivable situation).

**4:26 Jerusalem that is above.** The heavenly city that was thought to provide the pattern for the actual city. The heavenly Jerusalem is the real thing, uncorrupted and perfect (see also Heb. 12:22; Rev. 3:12; 21:2,9–14). Here it stands for the Christian church.

**4:27** Isaiah was celebrating the fact that though the children of Zion (Jerusalem) had been carried into captivity in Babylon, one day they would return and become more numerous than before. So, too, the Gentiles were spiritually barren but are now producing spiritual fruit.

**4:29** In 1 Thessalonians 2:14–16, Paul mentions Jewish persecution of Christians.

**4:30** When Sarah sees Ishmael playing with Isaac, she recalls her jealousy of Hagar and so tells Abraham to drive them from the camp. Paul's point is that "legal bondage and spiritual freedom cannot coexist" (Bruce). Paul is not considering the question of Sarah's jealousy or her unkindness.

## Religious People Are Not Immune to Sin

Paul is saying an interesting thing here: "Just because you are religious is no guarantee that you are righteous." Within a religious system like Judaism in which ritual and behavior were so important, it was easy to lapse into a false security that just because you did all the right things, kept all the feasts, and performed all the rituals, God *had* to approve of you. In fact, as Jesus showed (and as indeed the Old Testament said when one looked carefully) God did not want just outward obedience (though he did want this). He also wanted inward purity. And no one (except Jesus) has ever been able to live a life that perfect.

This is a problem for religious folks. At times while their outer lives might be a model of rectitude, their inner, secret lives are a jungle of desires and hostilities. The reason is clear—we are all "fallen" people. There is an alien principle within us that keeps twisting things around. At times even our most selfless acts of giving can be, if we are honest, sources of pride or some other not so good thing.

Religious people like the first-century Jews and like us modern Christians need to know that we can never earn God's favor. We simply are not good enough nor consistent enough, even when we are trying hard to do what is right. Of course this discovery is a great relief. We can then own our failures and admit our faults, knowing that God is not going to "get us" because of them. He already knows what we are like. This is why salvation (right standing before God) is a gift received by faith and not a wage earned by activity.

# 11 Freedom in Christ—Gal. 5:1–15

## THREE-PART AGENDA

**ICE-BREAKER**
15 Minutes

**BIBLE STUDY**
30 Minutes

**CARING TIME**
15–45 Minutes

 *LEADER: To help you identify an Apprentice / Leader and the people who might form the core of a new small group, see the listing of ice-breakers on page M7 of the center section.*

## TO BEGIN THE BIBLE STUDY TIME
(Choose 1 or 2)

1. If you were free to do anything you want tomorrow, what would you do?

2. How do you feel and react when others cut in on you—while driving, waiting in line, speaking, etc.?

3. Who in this group deserves the award for best honoring the commandment—"Love your neighbor as yourself"?

## READ SCRIPTURE & DISCUSS
(If you don't have time for all the questions in this section, conclude the Bible Study [30 min.] by answering question #7.)

1. When you first moved away from home, what did "freedom" mean to you? Free to do what? Free from what?

2. What does it mean to be "free" in Christ (v. 1)?

3. Why does Paul make such a big deal about circumcision? Since our own efforts and achievements aren't the way to God, what is (vv. 5–6)?

4. How can the "yeast" (v. 9) of false teaching be avoided? What "tough love" is Paul demonstrating toward those who are spreading these falsehoods?

### Freedom in Christ

**5** *It is for freedom that Christ has set us free. Stand firm, then, and do not let yourselves be burdened again by a yoke of slavery.*

*²Mark my words! I, Paul, tell you that if you let yourselves be circumcised, Christ will be of no value to you at all. ³Again I declare to every man who lets himself be circumcised that he is obligated to obey the whole law. ⁴You who are trying to be justified by law have been alienated from Christ; you have fallen away from grace. ⁵But by faith we eagerly await through the Spirit the righteousness for which we hope. ⁶For in Christ Jesus neither circumcision nor uncircumcision has any value. The only thing that counts is faith expressing itself through love.*

*⁷You were running a good race. Who cut in on you and kept you from obeying the truth? ⁸That kind of persuasion does not come from the one who calls you. ⁹"A little yeast works through the whole batch of dough." ¹⁰I am confident in the Lord that you will take no other view. The one who is throwing you into confusion will pay the penalty, whoever he may be. ¹¹Brothers, if I am still preaching circumcision, why am I still being persecuted? In that case the offense of the cross has been abolished. ¹²As for those agitators, I wish they would go the whole way and emasculate themselves!*

*¹³You, my brothers, were called to be free. But do not use your freedom to indulge the sinful nature*ᵃ*; rather, serve one another in love. ¹⁴The entire law is summed up in a single command: "Love your neighbor as yourself."*ᵇ *¹⁵If you keep on biting and devouring each other, watch out or you will be destroyed by each other.*

ᵃ*13 Or the flesh; also in verses 16,17,19 and 24*     ᵇ*14 Lev. 19:18*

5. When have you gotten off the track in the "good race" of the Christian life? Who or what cut in on you and sidetracked you?

6. What does verse 13 say to those who think their freedom in Christ allows them to do anything they want?

7. Although we have been liberated from spiritual slavery, what kind of servants do we become (vv. 13–15)? How can you incorporate this servanthood more into your own life?

## CARING TIME
(Choose 1 or 2 of these questions before closing in prayer.)

1. Who would you choose as the leader if this group "gave birth" to a new small group? Who else would you choose to be a part of the leadership core for a new group?

2. How has God been at work in your life this past week?

3. What prayer requests do you have for this week?

**5:1** Paul sums up the meaning of the allegory from the previous passage: as children of the free woman (4:31), they must tenaciously resist the loss of that freedom.

**5:2** *I, Paul.* Paul speaks with the full weight of his apostolic authority.

*circumcised.* The removal of the foreskin of the male genital organ, normally on the eighth day after birth. This rite was established by God as a sign of the covenant (Gen. 17).

**5:3** If the male members of the church allow themselves to be circumcised (and believe this to be a vital and necessary part of their salvation), they in essence acknowledge the binding quality of the whole Law over their lives.

*lets himself.* A baby has no choice. Others decide to circumcise him. But for adults, it requires a conscious choice to undergo this surgical procedure.

**5:4** A person can seek right standing before God either by legal works or by grace—not by both. Grace is not *grace* (a freely given gift) if there is any requirement at all for receiving it.

*trying to be justified.* Paul has said repeatedly that it is impossible to gain right standing via the Law (see Rom. 11:7). The only thing the Law brings (in this context) is a curse (3:10–14).

**5:5** *Spirit.* It is the Holy Spirit who fosters such assurances of acquittal.

*hope.* The Christian can confidently expect a positive verdict on the Judgment Day. To have such a hope in advance of the event brings great liberty and rejoicing. This stands in contrast to the anxiety of one who is never sure if they have done quite enough "good works" or have been faithful to all points of the Law. Such people (the legalists) will not know until the Last Day if they have made it into God's kingdom or not (Rom. 2:5–16).

**5:6** *neither circumcision nor uncircumcision.* Neither is a virtue. Christianity has room for all people. Circumcision is the wrong issue. Faith, hope and love (vv. 5–6) are the issues.

*faith / love.* Faith is the root, love is the fruit (Bruce).

> *The Christian can confidently expect a positive verdict on the Judgment Day. To have such a hope in advance of the event brings great liberty and rejoicing.*

**5:7** *running a good race.* In fact, those who would be most open to the appeals of the Judaizers would be the sincere, dedicated Galatians who wanted nothing more than to please God. But as relatively new Christians, they would not know that they were being diverted into a legalism that led away from Christ.

*race.* Paul uses an athletic metaphor to describe what happened to the Galatians.

*cut in on you.* A vivid word originally referring to the breaking up of roads by armies so as to hinder the progress of the enemy; it came to carry the idea of cutting in front of a runner to trip him up.

*the truth.* The Gospel (2:5,14).

**5:8** If such persuasion does not come from God (who is the one who calls them), the implication is that it comes from Satan (no matter who the agents are).

**5:9** A proverb, the point of which is that legalism no more belongs in the church than leaven had any right to be in a Jewish home on Passover Eve (Bruce). Such a wrong idea can corrupt the whole community (see 1 Cor. 5:6).

**5:10** Despite the magnitude of the problem, Paul does not despair—not because he trusts in the ultimate goodness or wisdom of human beings, but because of his confidence in the Lord.

*whoever he may be.* Paul may not know the actual identity of the Judaizers.

**5:11** Paul replies to the allegation that he is preaching circumcision, a charge that was probably used to convince the Galatians to be circumcised.

*still.* The only time Paul might have preached circumcision was prior to his conversion when he was a Jewish evangelist. Or the reference may be to a misinterpretation of the circumcision of Timothy (he had a Jewish mother) or misunderstanding of the incident with Titus (2:1–3).

*persecuted.* If he had been preaching circumcision, then he would not have been harassed by the militants.

*the offense of the cross.* To the Jew it was scarcely comprehensible that one who was accursed as a result of hanging on the cross should be portrayed as the Messiah. For the Gentile, it seemed the height of folly that a convicted criminal who could not save himself could save them. Furthermore, "to be shut up to receiving salvation from the crucified one, if it is to be received at all, is an affront to all notions of self-pride and self-help—and for many people this remains a major stumbling block in the gospel of Christ crucified. If I myself can make some small contribution, something even so small as the acceptance of circumcision, then my self-esteem is uninjured" (Bruce).

*abolished.* If a person can earn salvation by circumcision and law-keeping, then a crucified savior is unnecessary (and so the offense and the persecution disappears).

**5:12** In a rich (albeit coarse) jibe at the Judaizers, Paul suggests that if they are so preoccupied with circumcision, they really ought to take their knives and make eunuchs out of themselves!

**5:13–15** In typical fashion, Paul moves from the theological to the practical. His doctrinal case complete, he hastens to show what these truths mean in the life of the believer.

**5:13** *free. But ...* What Paul has written about freedom from the Law could be misunderstood to be a license to indulge in all of one's appetites, and certainly he does not mean that. So he begins this new section on Christian living by examining the use of freedom. What Paul is calling for is responsible freedom, which, as he says, is the freedom to serve others in love.

*freedom.* Christian freedom stands between the extreme of legal bondage (life lived within a web of requirements—v. 1) and the other extreme of unbridled indulgence (life lived without regard to any rules). Paul has already said that no one can be truly free until Christ takes away their burden of guilt (Christ frees a person from the power of the Law). Now he will show that one also needs to be freed from the power of sinful desires, which comes by the infilling of the Holy Spirit.

> **Faith is the root, love is the fruit.**

*the sinful nature.* The self-serving, self-seeking, self-indulgent aspect of human nature (see 5:19–21 for a partial list of its works).

*serve.* Literally, serve as slaves. The only form of slavery that is compatible with freedom is self-giving to others.

**5:14** Paul echoes the teaching of Jesus in this summary of the Law (Mark 12:28–31).

**5:15** Paul uses the vivid image of a pack of wild animals tearing one another to pieces to describe the effect of the false teachers.

# 12 Life by the Spirit—Gal. 5:16–26

## THREE-PART AGENDA

| ICE-BREAKER | BIBLE STUDY | CARING TIME |
|---|---|---|
| 15 Minutes | 30 Minutes | 15–45 Minutes |

> **LEADER:** *Has your group discussed its plans on what to study after this course is finished? What about the mission project described on page M6 in the center section?*

## TO BEGIN THE BIBLE STUDY TIME
(Choose 1 or 2)

1. On a scale of 0 (none) to 10 (tons), how many "wild oats" did you sow in your youth?

2. What are you more likely to get hooked on: Junk food? TV? The Internet? Other?

3. Who or what influences you the most in: The clothes you wear? The music you listen to? Your values?

## READ SCRIPTURE & DISCUSS
(If you don't have time for all the questions in this section, conclude the Bible Study [30 min.] by answering question #7.)

1. What motivates you to live a good life?

2. Over and over Paul has warned the Galatians about being enslaved to legalism. What does he warn them about being enslaved to in this passage?

3. What two things are in conflict with each other (v. 17)? If we are made alive by the Spirit, why do we still struggle with sin?

Life by the Spirit

*¹⁶So I say, live by the Spirit, and you will not gratify the desires of the sinful nature. ¹⁷For the sinful nature desires what is contrary to the Spirit, and the Spirit what is contrary to the sinful nature. They are in conflict with each other, so that you do not do what you want. ¹⁸But if you are led by the Spirit, you are not under law.*

*¹⁹The acts of the sinful nature are obvious: sexual immorality, impurity and debauchery; ²⁰idolatry and witchcraft; hatred, discord, jealousy, fits of rage, selfish ambition, dissensions, factions ²¹and envy; drunkenness, orgies, and the like. I warn you, as I did before, that those who live like this will not inherit the kingdom of God.*

*²²But the fruit of the Spirit is love, joy, peace, patience, kindness, goodness, faithfulness, ²³gentleness and self-control. Against such things there is no law. ²⁴Those who belong to Christ Jesus have crucified the sinful nature with its passions and desires. ²⁵Since we live by the Spirit, let us keep in step with the Spirit. ²⁶Let us not become conceited, provoking and envying each other.*

4. Can a person who lives according to the "acts of the sinful nature" in verses 19–21 be a true Christian (see third note on v. 21)?

5. How can you and God's Spirit weed out the sinful nature and grow the fruit of the Spirit?

6. Which of the fruit of the Spirit (vv. 22–23) are blossoming in your life right now? Which are still in the bud?

7. What is the biggest change that being a Christian has made in your life? How do you sense God calling you to change your lifestyle?

## CARING TIME
(Answer all the questions that follow, then close in prayer.)

1. Next week will be your last session in this study. How would you like to celebrate: A dinner? A party? Other?

2. What is the next step for this group: Start a new group? Continue with another study?

3. How can the group pray for you this week?

(If the group plans to continue, see the back inside cover of this book for what is available from Serendipity.)

**5:16** Having warned against losing one's freedom by submitting to circumcision (5:1–2), Paul now warns about losing freedom by submitting to sinful desires.

***live by the Spirit.*** Literally, walk by the Spirit; i.e., let the way you live, your conduct, be directed by the Holy Spirit. It is the Holy Spirit, not the Law, who will bring about a moral lifestyle.

**5:17** Two principles are at war in the Christian's life. "But the believer is not the helpless battle ground of two opposing forces. If he yields to the flesh, he is enslaved by it, but if he obeys the prompting of the Spirit, he is liberated" (Bruce).

**5:18** The Spirit is as opposed to the Law as to the sinful nature (vv. 16–17). To be led by the Spirit enables a person to resist sinful desire. To be under Law, however, gives a person no protection at all against such inner cravings.

**5:19** ***acts of the sinful nature.*** To illustrate specifically the sort of lifestyle that emerges when the sinful nature is allowed its sway, Paul produces a representative list of vices.

**5:20** ***idolatry.*** The worship of any idol, be it a carved image of God (a statue) or an abstract substitute for God (a status symbol). An idol is identified as such because when faced with a choice, a person will follow its leading. Money, for example, becomes an idol when to gain it a person will do anything.

***witchcraft.*** *Pharmakeia* is literally "the use of drugs," which was often associated with the practice of sorcery.

***hatred.*** This is the underlying political, social and religious hostility which drives individuals and communities apart.

***discord.*** This is the type of contention which leads to factions.

***selfish ambition.*** This word came to refer to anyone who worked only for their own good and not for the benefit of others.

*FRUIT OF THE SPIRIT: These are the traits which characterize the child of God. The list is representative and not exhaustive:*

**LOVE:** *Agape; in contrast, there is eros (sexual love), philos (warm feelings to friends and family), and storge (family affection). None of these adequately describe the self-giving, active benevolence that is meant to characterize Christian love, hence the repeated use in the New Testament of agape—a relatively uncommon word redefined by Christians to bear this meaning.*

**JOY:** *The Greek word is chara, and comes from the same root as "grace" (charis). It is not based on earthly things or human achievement; it is a gift from God based on a right relationship with him.*

**PEACE:** *The prime meaning of this word is not negative ("an absence of conflict"), but positive ("the presence of that which brings wholeness and well-being").*

**PATIENCE:** *This is the ability to be steadfast with people, refusing to give up on them.*

**KINDNESS:** *This is the compassionate use of strength for the good of another.*

**GOODNESS:** *This implies moral purity which reflects the character of God.*

**FAITHFULNESS:** *This is to be reliable and trustworthy.*

**GENTLENESS:** *According to Aristotle, this is the virtue that lies between excessive proneness to anger and the inability to be angry; it implies control of oneself.*

**SELF-CONTROL:** *This is control of one's sensual passions, rather than control of one's anger (as in gentleness).*

**factions.** This means the party spirit which leads people to regard those with whom they disagree as enemies.

**5:21 drunkenness.** In the first century, diluted wine was drunk regularly by all ages, but drunkenness was not common and was condemned (because it was thought to turn a person into a beast).

**and the like.** The list is representative, not exhaustive—touching, in order, upon the sins of sensuality, idolatry, social dissension, and intemperance.

**not inherit.** The issue here is not sins into which one falls, but sin as a lifestyle. These are evidence of a life not controlled by the Spirit, and therefore the implication is that such a person has not been born from above and become a child of God.

**5:22 fruit of the Spirit.** These are the traits which characterize the child of God. Again, the list is representative and not exhaustive.

**love.** Agape; in contrast, there is eros (sexual love), philos (warm feelings to friends and family), and storge (family affection). None of these adequately describe the self-giving, active benevolence that is meant to characterize Christian love, hence the repeated use in the New Testament of agape—a relatively uncommon word redefined by Christians to bear this meaning.

**joy.** The Greek word is chara, and comes from the same root as "grace" (charis). It is not based on earthly things or human achievement; it is a gift from God based on a right relationship with him.

**peace.** The prime meaning of this word is not negative ("an absence of conflict"), but positive ("the presence of that which brings wholeness and well-being").

**patience.** This is the ability to be steadfast with people, refusing to give up on them.

**kindness.** This is the compassionate use of strength for the good of another.

**goodness.** This implies moral purity which reflects the character of God.

**faithfulness.** This is to be reliable and trustworthy.

**5:23 gentleness.** According to Aristotle, this is the virtue that lies between excessive proneness to anger and the inability to be angry; it implies control of oneself.

**self-control.** This is control of one's sensual passions, rather than control of one's anger (as in gentleness).

**there is no law.** While it is possible to legislate certain forms of behavior, one cannot command love, joy, peace, etc. These are each gifts of God's grace. With this list of qualities one moves into a whole new realm of reality, well beyond the sphere of Law.

**5:24 have crucified the sinful nature.** It is via the cross that a person dies to the power of the Law (2:19). Paul indicates here that in the same way, a person also dies to the power of their sinful nature. The verb indicates that this is not something done to the Christian but by the Christian. The Christian actively and deliberately has repented of (turned away from) the old wayward patterns of life.

**5:25 live by the Spirit.** In the same way that the death of the ego (the "I" principle) is replaced by the mind of Christ (2:20), here Paul indicates that the death of the sinful nature is replaced by the life of the Spirit.

**let us.** Having just indicated that the Christian does live by the power of the Spirit, Paul (in characteristic fashion) balances off that indicative ("this is the way things are") with an imperative ("now you do this"). "Walking by the Spirit is the outward manifestation, in action and speech, of living by the Spirit. Living by the Spirit is the root; walking by the Spirit is the fruit and that fruit is nothing less than the practical reproduction of the character (and therefore conduct) of Christ in the lives of his people" (Bruce).

# 13 Doing Good—Galatians 6:1–18

## THREE-PART AGENDA

**ICE-BREAKER**
15 Minutes

**BIBLE STUDY**
30 Minutes

**CARING TIME**
15–45 Minutes

 *LEADER: Check page M7 of the center section for a good ice-breaker for this last session.*

## TO BEGIN THE BIBLE STUDY TIME
(Choose 1 or 2)

1. How are you at growing things? What kind of garden have you tended?

2. What is one good deed you've done recently that you would love to boast about if the group would let you?

3. In what areas do you tend to compare yourself to others: Looks? Career? Lifestyle? Money? Other?

## READ SCRIPTURE & DISCUSS
(If you don't have time for all the questions in this section, conclude the Bible Study [30 min.] by answering question #7.)

1. How has this group, or someone in the group, been a blessing to you over the course of this study?

2. As brothers and sisters in Christ, what responsibilities do we have for each other?

3. What sorts of burdens do your family and friends carry? How do you (or could you) help them with these burdens?

4. What is the gist of Paul's teaching on the Spirit-filled life (vv. 7–10)? Where in your life do you need to sow to please the Spirit?

## Doing Good to All

**6** *Brothers, if someone is caught in a sin, you who are spiritual should restore him gently. But watch yourself, or you also may be tempted. ²Carry each other's burdens, and in this way you will fulfill the law of Christ. ³If anyone thinks he is something when he is nothing, he deceives himself. ⁴Each one should test his own actions. Then he can take pride in himself, without comparing himself to somebody else, ⁵for each one should carry his own load.*

*⁶Anyone who receives instruction in the word must share all good things with his instructor.*

*⁷Do not be deceived: God cannot be mocked. A man reaps what he sows. ⁸The one who sows to please his sinful nature, from that nature*ᵃ *will reap destruction; the one who sows to please the Spirit, from the Spirit will reap eternal life. ⁹Let us not become weary in doing good, for at the proper time we will reap a harvest if we do not give up. ¹⁰Therefore, as we have opportunity, let us do good to all people, especially to those who belong to the family of believers.*

## Not Circumcision but a New Creation

*¹¹See what large letters I use as I write to you with my own hand!*

*¹²Those who want to make a good impression outwardly are trying to compel you to be circumcised. The only reason they do this is to avoid being persecuted for the cross of Christ. ¹³Not even those who are circumcised obey the law, yet they want you to be circumcised that they may boast about your flesh. ¹⁴May I never boast except in the cross of our Lord Jesus Christ, through which*ᵇ *the world has been crucified to me, and I to the world. ¹⁵Neither circumcision nor uncircumcision means anything; what counts is a new creation. ¹⁶Peace and mercy to all who follow this rule, even to the Israel of God.*

*¹⁷Finally, let no one cause me trouble, for I bear on my body the marks of Jesus.*

*¹⁸The grace of our Lord Jesus Christ be with your spirit, brothers. Amen.*

ᵃ8 Or *his flesh, from the flesh*        ᵇ14 Or *whom*

5. What does it mean to have the cross as your model in daily life? What does it mean to "boast" in the cross of Jesus (v. 14)? Is this boasting a part of your life?

6. In this study of Galatians, what has been the key thing you learned?

7. On a scale of 1 (baby steps) to 10 (giant leaps), how has your relationship with God progressed over the last three months?

## CARING TIME
(Answer all the questions that follow, then close in prayer.)

1. What will you remember most about this group?

2. What has the group decided to do next? What is the next step for you personally?

3. How would you like the group to continue to pray for you?

# Notes—Galatians 6:1–18

**6:1–2** Paul immediately applies what he taught in 5:13–26, beginning with the case of a church member who has given in to temptation. Contrary to what some might expect, he does not counsel harshness but rather burden-bearing love.

**6:1** *a sin.* A temporary lapse (as over against an active lifestyle).

*you who are spiritual.* Those whose lives bear the mark of the Spirit. This is not a clique of "special" Christians but is a call to all Christians (5:24–25).

*restore.* A medical term, used to describe the setting of a fractured bone. The verb tense (in Greek) implies that this is not a single act but a continuous action.

*gently.* This is a fruit of the Spirit (5:23). The temptation may be to display overt disapproval and censorious judgment on the offender, but Paul counsels otherwise.

*watch yourself.* No one is beyond temptation; all are vulnerable, so no one has any basis for self-righteousness. To watch means not simply to glance casually, but to gaze with concentration (such as an archer concentrating on a target prior to loosing an arrow). This is active self-examination. This concept is picked up again in verse 4 in the idea of testing one's actions.

**6:2** This is the general principle which lies behind the specific instruction in verse 1.

*Carry each other's burdens.* Mutual burden-bearing lies at the heart of Christian fellowship.

*burdens.* A heavy, crushing weight which a single individual cannot carry.

*law of Christ.* The law of love (5:14), which stands in sharp contrast to the Law as practiced in first-century Israel. It involves submission to a *person* (Jesus), not to a *code* (the Law of Moses).

**6:3** A warning against spiritual pride. A sense of self-importance would make it difficult for such a person to bear another's burden (much less to restore gently the person overtaken in sin).

**6:4** *Each one should test.* This is an individual act. There is no "committee on standards" set up to evaluate individual Christians. The word for *test* is the same one used to describe the testing of metals to see if they are pure.

*his own actions.* The subject of the self-assessment is not inner feelings or ideological commitments, but measurable activity. The question is: how is my life being lived? Note also that it is one's own actions, not those of other people, that are to be examined.

*without comparing.* The temptation is to say, "Oh, I'm not so bad. Look at what so-and-so does," thus deflecting true insight into oneself and giving rise to false pride.

**6:5** *load.* This is not the same as the crushing burden in verse 2. Rather, the word is used to describe the small individual pack a hiker or soldier carries. This is the same word used by Jesus in Matthew 11:30 to describe the burden (load) of his yoke.

**6:6** As an example of burden-bearing in action, Paul cites the obligation of the church to support its teachers (Matt. 10:10; 1 Cor. 9:14). The instructor lifts the burden of ignorance and misunderstanding from the shoulders of the congregation, while they in turn share in the material support of the teacher (lifting their burden to provide daily sustenance).

> *The temptation is to say, "Oh, I'm not so bad. Look at what so-and-so does," thus deflecting true insight into oneself and giving rise to false pride.*

**6:7** *mocked.* This is derived from the word for "snout," and means "to turn up one's nose" at somebody in contempt.

**6:8–9** "What the apostle is saying is that if we base our lives on the principle that self comes first we shall end up, rotten to the core, in spiritual death. If

60

we let the Spirit of Jesus guide our behavior, the end-product is life as God meant it to be, life lived in such a relationship to God that the death of the body cannot destroy it" (Neil).

**6:9 give up.** That is, lose heart. The idea is of fatigue, such as laborers in the field might feel under the blazing sun. Still they must keep on gathering in the harvest.

**6:11** Paul takes pen in hand and writes the final paragraph of his letter, having dictated it up to this point. He calls attention to this, because his letter would most likely be read aloud to the church and people would not see for themselves the change in handwriting.

**large letters.** For emphasis' sake, probably.

**6:12 avoid being persecuted.** The motivation behind the Judaizers is self-interest. If they can persuade the Gentile Christians to be circumcised, they will avoid reprisals by the militants in Jerusalem (see first note on 2:12 on page 28).

**for the cross of Christ.** To these zealots, the cross was offensive, since it excluded the need for the Law of Moses.

**6:13** The concern of the Judaizers is not just "zeal for the Lord" (as they might protest), but so that they can boast of the many that follow their teaching.

**obey the law.** Paul is probably not pointing a finger at specific examples of law-breaking on their part, but at the impossibility for anyone to keep the Law.

**6:14 boast ... in the cross.** To both Jew and Greek, a cross was a symbol of horror. Polite Romans would not even mention it, and orthodox Jews saw it as a sign of God's curse. But this is what Paul boasts in!

**the world.** The world system of values, ideas and powers that is opposed to God.

> *No one is beyond temptation; all are vulnerable, so no one has any basis for self-righteousness.*

**crucified to me.** Paul is dead to the influence of these anti-God ideas and powers. The crucifixion of Christ has become the pattern on which his life is based (2:20).

**6:15** Here Paul echoes his summary statement in 5:6. External conformity to Jewish tradition (and, by extension, any religious tradition) is simply beside the point. What matters is whether or not one has been renewed by the Spirit of God.

**new creation.** While the full benefits and extent of this new creation will be experienced only in the age to come, believers experience it in part here and now, through the Holy Spirit.

**6:16 the Israel of God.** In this phrase, Paul redefined the very nature of what it means to be God's people. It is no longer, as the Jews had long thought, a matter of ethnicity. Instead, the true Israel, the true people of God, are all those who are part of this new creation which has been brought about by Jesus. One becomes a part of the new Israel not through circumcision and adherence to Jewish customs, but through faith in Christ expressed in acts of love toward others (5:6). Those who follow this "rule" will experience God's peace and mercy.

**6:17 marks of Jesus.** In contrast to the now meaningless mark of circumcision (v. 15a), Paul bears

> *If we let the Spirit of Jesus guide our behavior, the end-product is life as God meant it to be, life lived in such a relationship to God that the death of the body cannot destroy it.*

# Notes—(cont.)

scars as a result of his service for Christ. An example of this would be from the stoning at Lystra (Acts 14:19), which Paul's readers would have known about (since this letter was addressed to the church there). In the first century, slaves were branded with their owner's mark. In a real sense, Paul is the slave of Christ. In certain pagan cults, devotees were tattooed to show to whom they belonged. Paul's scars indicate his allegiance to Jesus.

**6:18** Paul ends with a warm, personal note. His anger is done with. He has said what must be said. He concludes by recalling their common kinship in Christ.

## Fellowship in the Early Church

The quality of fellowship in the early church was both striking and appealing—striking because it contrasted so sharply with what occurred in other institutions, and appealing because its very quality made men and women hungry to be a part of it. At the heart of this new fellowship was the eradication of those barriers that had divided the ancient world: race, class and gender. "There is neither Jew nor Greek, slave nor free, male nor female, for you are all one in Christ Jesus" is how Paul expresses this truth in Galatians 3:28.

What created this new unity? At its core, of course, was the transforming death and resurrection of Jesus Christ which drew people together into new relationships. This fellowship was then deepened as Christians "devoted themselves to the apostles' teaching and to the fellowship, to the breaking of bread and to prayer" (Acts 2:42). The unity was maintained because problems and aberrations were not allowed to disrupt the fellowship. In Galatians 2:11–21 and elsewhere Paul, as well as the other apostles, deals swiftly and directly with such problems lest they take root and destroy this new unity. (Adapted from *Evangelism in the Early Church* by Michael Green, Eerdmans Publishing, pp. 180–183).

# Acknowledgments

The central source consulted for the Notes in this study was F. F. Bruce's *Commentary on Galatians* (New International Greek Testament Series), Grand Rapids, MI: Wm. B. Eerdmans Publishing Co., 1982. In addition, good use was made of *The Letter of Paul to the Galatians* (The Cambridge Bible Commentary) by William Neil (Cambridge: The University Press, 1967) and *Galatians* (The New Century Bible Commentary series) by Donald Guthrie (Grand Rapids, MI: Wm. B. Eerdmans Publishing Co., 1981). Reference was also made to *Only One Way: The Message of Galatians* (The Bible Speaks Today series) by John R. W. Stott (Downers Grove, IL: InterVarsity Press, 1968); *Galatians* (*Hermeneia*) by Hans Dieter Betz (Philadelphia: Fortress Press, 1979); *2 Corinthians and Galatians* (Neighborhood Bible Studies) by Marilyn Kunz and Catherine Schell (Wheaton, IL: Tyndale House Publishers, 1975); and *St. Paul's Epistle to the Galatians,* by J. B. Lightfoot (Grand Rapids, MI: Zondervan); as well as the standard lexicons, dictionaries, etc.

# Caring Time Notes